THE Seven Commandments of Discipleship

Other Books by Frank P. DeSiano, C.S.P.
Published by Paulist Press

Presenting the Catholic Faith

Sowing New Seed:
Directions for Evangelization Today

The Evangelizing Catholic:
A Practical Handbook for Reaching Out

Católicos Evangelizadores:
Un Manual Práctico para Extender la Fe

Coauthored with Kenneth Boyack, C.S.P.:

Creating the Evangelizing Parish

Discovering My Experience of God:
Awareness and Witness

Descubrir Mi Experiencia de Dios:
Conciencia y Testimonio

Coauthored with Susan Blum Gerding:

Lay Ministers, Lay Disciples:
Evangelizing Power in the Parish

THE Seven Commandments of Discipleship

What God Asks of Us

Frank P. DeSiano, C.S.P.

Paulist Press
New York/Mahwah, N.J.

Scripture extracts are taken from the New Revised Standard Version, Copyright © 1989, by the Division of Christian Education of the National Council of the Churches of Christ in the United States of America and reprinted by permission of the publisher.

Cover design by Sharyn Banks
Book design by Lynn Else

Library of Congress Cataloging-in-Publication Data

DeSiano, Frank P.
The seven commandments of discipleship : what God asks of us / Frank P. DeSiano.
p. cm.
ISBN 0-8091-4166-3 (alk. paper)
1. Christian life—Catholic authors. I. Title.
BX2350.3 .D47 2003
248.4′82—dc21

2003004574

Published by Paulist Press
997 Macarthur Boulevard
Mahwah, New Jersey 07430

www.paulistpress.com

Printed and bound in the United States of America

Contents

With gratitude for much help from
Edwin, Joe, Mike, Bill, and Sharon

In Memory of a True Disciple,
Hannah Campbell

Introduction

So what does God expect of us?

We've all known people whom we have considered "saints" often because they struck us as so scrupulous, so rigidly entrenched in their faith, that they frightened us. What better way to deal with that fright, that intensity, than to put them into special category? "They are saints."

Far more often, however, we have known people who in some way call themselves religious, affixing some kind of denominational or spiritual label on themselves, but they have little burning interest in God, faith, or even other people. Perhaps they worship once or twice a year, attend weddings or funerals, or know how to say a prayer in a time of stress or need. But that's about as far as it goes. When asked, however, they still describe themselves as religious.

Quite unlike those scrupulous folk we might style as "saints," these people help give religion the faceless blur that modern society likes. God-lite. Religion-soft. Faith-comfortable. Sacrifice-nil.

Between these two religious extremes, though, where do we find ourselves? More pointedly, where do we think God wants us to be?

What Might God Want?

Our images of God can often arise from our own different moods, our styles. We shift between a God whose jealousy and severity would make the most hardened sinner cringe, and a God whose folksy, easy-going ways would ask hardly anything of us. We get used to one style, and then start longing for the other. We cannot settle on one image.

Is God the giver of laws, the certain punisher of sinners, the relentless seeker of justice such that God seems to be fixated—and frightening? We dare not approach this God; to keep God's laws and avoid trouble make up our spiritual project (see Exod 20:18–20). Or is God the sweet forgiver, our best friend and pal, more nonjudgmental than the best therapist, the almost foolish father who throws himself at the child who has wasted everything on silly quests for pleasure, as the parable of the Prodigal son seems to suggest (see Luke 15:20)?

Although the Scriptures themselves might appear to be here-and-there when it comes to reflecting on what God demands of us, in certain places they seem to speak quite clearly. The book of Deuteronomy, which is the closing book of what the Jewish people call the Torah, explores in a fundamental way the relationship between God and God's people. That relationship, based on the covenant God made with the Jewish people, can be perhaps essentially expressed by the notion of *faithful loyalty*. God will be faithfully loyal to the Jewish people; God expects their faithful loyalty in return.

One particular verse of that book, in the form of Moses talking to the people, puts it pretty squarely: "So now, O Israel, what does the LORD your God require of you? Only to fear the LORD your God, to walk in his ways, to love him, to serve the LORD your God with all your heart and with all your soul, and to keep the commandments of the LORD your God and his decrees that I am commanding you today, for your own well-being" (Deut 10:12–13).

Sentences like this initially encourage us because the requirement of God seems so simply put, but once we begin to explore its meaning, the sentence reads like God is asking everything of us. What God asks in this passage seems well beyond the Ten Commandments that Moses gave to the Jewish people. Is not God asking the people to serve him with all their heart and soul? What an inexhaustible requirement that would be. After all, the only being we automatically love with all our heart and soul is...ourselves!

We are consoled, then, when the prophet Micah seems to soften God's requirement: "...[A]nd what does the LORD require of you but to do justice, and to love kindness, and to walk humbly with your God?" (Mic 6:8) This seems far more digestible to us. Do not we all love kindness and want what is right? And who can walk arrogantly before God? No one that we know.

But the seeming simplicity of Micah's sentence is quite deceptive. Because with only a little following of the Lord, we soon see that pursuing justice, or even recognizing kindness, first demands a commitment of all our heart and soul. Because without that kind of commitment, we keep cutting corners on what is just, and lowering the standards of kindness. Before the face of God, is that not sheer arrogance?

Jesus put the demands even more starkly for those who would follow him. "If any want to become my followers, let them deny themselves and take up their cross and follow me. For those who want to save their life will lose it, and those who lose their life for my sake, and for the sake of the gospel, will save it" (Mark 8:34–35).

This requirement seems to be of an entirely different order than that of Micah, or even Deuteronomy's command to serve God with all our heart and soul. We might happily endure some particular loss or pain if we have to because of our love for someone. But to "take up" a cross? To deny our very selves? To lose our lives as a way of saving our lives? This seems like certain defeat. Can God be asking this of us?

Jesus' life can be interpreted as living out totally the covenant relationship that God established with the chosen. The cross was Christ's personal living out of what it means to serve with everything one has. His death was the acceptance of an injustice for the sake of a greater justice—clarifying our fundamental relationship with God, justifying us through the absolute sign of forgiveness that his death portrays. So Jesus loves the Father with all his heart, soul, mind, and strength, even to the end. And how could one walk more humbly with God than by taking those burdened steps of Christ's final walk to Golgotha where, in shame, he embodied a total love for God, in his own name and in ours as well? Jesus responds to all God's requirements in his life, death, and resurrection.

What does God ask of us? What does Jesus require of us? Quite simply, that we come to love like Jesus loved, with the total freedom that constitutes his own spirituality, the inner dimension of his personal vision.

Another way of saying this is: Jesus asks us to be disciples, because disciples are those who follow him in living out the relationship with God which alone expresses the depth of love between God and God's people.

Many Christians are not used to thinking of themselves as disciples. For many centuries Christians have lived with a "double-decker" universe in which a few exceptional people (or a few exceptionally neurotic people) try to take faith seriously, leaving the rest of us to just plod along, half-Christian though we feel ourselves to be. The few who are heroes, after all, need many more of us to applaud them.

Yet does it have to be this way, a small group of the special surrounded by a larger crowd of the mediocre? Thérèse of Lisieux, the young nun whose life at the end of the nineteenth century seemed to set the tone for much of religious experience in the twentieth, helped to dismantle this double-decker universe. She concluded that, simple and secluded nun that she was, if she did every thing in her life, particularly the little things, with absolute love, then she would find the holiness of life that God asked of her. In her little book, *The Story of a Soul*, she shattered the rigidity of many of her contemporaries by making love the ultimate standard—and seeing love embodied in the heroics of daily life.

So if she could be a disciple, living as simply as she did, what about the rest of us? The world changing meeting of Catholic bishops that occurred at the Vatican in Rome in the mid-1960s continued dismantling the double-decker view of Christian life. Those bishops, when they wrote about the basic structure of Christian life, insisted that everyone is called to holiness. Not just the heroic, or the exceptional, or the peculiar, or the fanatical. "[A]ll the faithful, whatever their condition or state, are called by the Lord, each in his own way, to that perfect holiness whereby the Father Himself is perfect." (*Lumen Gentium*, 11)

The call to be a disciple, then, is the same call to be holy, to have our hearts shaped like the heart of Christ, our minds like his mind, our instincts like his instincts, our actions in the pattern of his.

The answer to our question, "What does God ask of us?" comes down to three words: To be disciples.

Discipleship and Commandments

Although this book basically explores various dimensions of discipleship, at this point it will help to sketch out some of the fundamental dimensions that discipleship entails, following the words Jesus gave us about how we are to love God and others (Mark 12:29–31).

The first involves our *minds*—that is to say, the consciousness that shapes our world. Disciples have God at the center of their world. Once having known God, one wants to know God even more, with all the nuances that "knowing God" points to. We want to take in God totally; or, to speak more correctly, we want to be taken over by God. We strain for anything that can unfold God's mystery for us, even as we know that this will only draw us more deeply into that mystery.

The second dimension involves our *hearts*—that is, the consequence of knowing God that leads us to adore, worship, and entrust ourselves to God—to live for God. When we understand prayer as the drama of our relationship with God, we see immediately that disciples, living from their hearts, cannot help but be people of prayer. Far more than the best human relationships of our lives, our relationship with God always grows deeper, often even when we can hardly see that growth.

The third dimension involves our *strength*—the way we live our relationship with God through our actions on behalf of others. How difficult in a world that revolves around "me being served," to see that we ourselves have to be primarily of service to others if we are at all going to reflect God in our own lives. To live for others, free of self-absorption, means having enormous resources of strength because God becomes our basic resource.

The final dimension speaks about *community*—loving others as we love ourselves—the human network in which disciples live and through which they alone can grow in the following of Jesus. As we live in a self-absorbed world, so also we live in a world that encourages privacy and isolation. One of the most frequently used religious phrases talks of Jesus as "my personal Lord and Savior," sometimes stated so as to distance a person from a church or community of faith. Disciples, however, realize that one cannot speak of the "personal" without also speaking of the communal—of the community that supports faith and the faith community that seeks to support the world. Mind, heart, strength, and community together say what discipleship means for people today

But why link the idea of discipleship with the notion of *commandment*? It must seem strange that the way chosen to elaborate the meaning of discipleship today is through the image of commandment—*The Seven Commandments of Discipleship*. After all, if the notions of community and service present difficulties for today's culture, the idea of commandment certainly doesn't make the situation any easier.

We so live in a rule-filled world that our greatest pleasure often is escaping rules. Children love amusement parks because they can fly higher, drive faster, spin more quickly, and drop more steeply than the normal rules of gravity would permit. And adults flock to movie houses as much for the escape from the boundaries of daily life as for the quality of the film. Through the screen, we older folk can also fly high, drive fast, spin quickly, and leap freely, at least in our imaginations. Not to mention shooting people, surviving great blasts, and fulfilling society's image of a great lover. The rules, for a few hours, are suspended.

To understand what a commandment is, however, we have to separate that idea from those about rules and laws, even though they may seem to mean the same thing. Rules and laws, as they are commonly conceived, provide guidelines that prevent clashes or disruptions, that provide for order or redress. Commandments do much more than this.

Commandments, when we think about it, get us in touch with our deepest values; they help us hold those values in times of stress and doubt. Providing boundaries for us is perhaps the least important thing commandments do, important as that may be. Showing us what lies in our deepest natures and expressing that in a set of values that must be upheld—this explains why Moses' tablets simply will not vanish from human consciousness. Life, truth, respect, faithful relationship, honesty, integrity, honor—all with God at the center of our lives—shows us who we are, or who we should be, in our human depths. These commandments cannot simply be rearranged or change in the way we might rewrite office rules or revise civil laws.

Commandments intimidate us, for sure, but not because they carry a big stick with which we can be beaten. They intimidate us by the sheer authority with which they are spoken, the authority written into our human existence itself. We do not shape commandments; they shape us.

Are there commandments of discipleship? Once we start to look at the basic framework that following Jesus involves, values that simply cannot be surmounted or dismissed do become clear.

We simply cannot get around them because they expose the inner nature of what it means to walk down Christ's path.

Before the 1960s, much of life had a clear structure, even if that clarity came mostly from a culture that had a powerful need at that time to organize itself. So parents, teachers, policemen, clergymen, and others who enshrined authority figures—many of them male—defined the universe of the child and, to a large extent, the adult world too. The police or teachers were like vicarious parents, unafraid to discipline in a world that prized discipline. Community mores seemed both solid and well accepted. Even a friend's parent would not fear to "lay down the law" for another child.

Since the 1960s, however, nothing has looked certain and everything has been questioned. The wondrous liberation that taught us how essential it is to question also made life's answers seem elusive or entirely missing. In fact, in contemporary experience, even believing we have a definitive answer often comes across to many as sheer arrogance.

As a result, the cultural structure of much modern life, and certainly much Christian life, has gotten hard to define. For Catholics to abstain from meat on Fridays and confess their sins on Saturdays, and for Protestants to read daily from their Bibles—to give very simple examples—seemed to provide a structure in the years before the 1960s. There were expectations. Now, however, nothing seems expected, necessary, or required. We make life up as we go along.

If God requires discipleship of us, however, then maybe there is a structure to Christian life, a basic outline that can hold our personal and communal Christian lives together.

When we speak of the commandments of discipleship, it helps us to get at that structure. If Christian life is just whatever we want it to be, then there isn't much to it. But if discipleship is a way of life that has observable elements to it, then there are things we need if we would follow down the path of Jesus.

This book points to some of the structure of Christian life today, in the twenty-first century, when the world is declared both "postmodern" and "post-Christian." The one phrase means that we cannot be sure of anything; the other means that, whoever Jesus was, he's not central for us today. Yet within this postmodern and post-Christian world stir powerful, widespread movements through which people seek a spiritual base—and the image of Jesus Christ simply will not dissolve.

In a world in which so many people exhaust themselves asking what it is they want, pursuing one fad after another, the question of what-God-wants demands an answer, particularly from those people who have truly sought—from those who have sought with all one's heart and soul, from those who have earnestly pursued justice and striven to walk humbly, from those who have renounced self and selfishness.

Surprisingly, after the debris of decades of self-doubt, the world seems filled with believers who are ready to become the disciples they were called to be.

Chapter One

You Shall Dwell in the Word of God

So what does God ask of us?

> Hear, O Israel: The Lord is our God, the Lord alone. You shall love the Lord your God with all your heart, and with all your soul, and with all your might. Keep these words that I am commanding you today in your heart. Recite them to your children and talk about them when you are at home and when you are away, when you lie down and when you rise. Bind them as a sign on your hand, fix them as an emblem on your forehead, and write them on the doorposts of your house and on your gates. (Deut 6:4–8)

Perhaps no generation in the history of the world has been as self-conscious as ours. Far and beyond individual therapy, people of all levels and backgrounds seem obsessed with what is going on inside their heads. Our radio programs beam out advice to help the distressed adjust to one or another hardship; the nightly news has a new result from some just-completed study showing us how to modify our inner feelings in some way and thereby totally change our lives. Young people strive to find themselves, as if they themselves were some lost, distant, but valuable object. Older folk dialogue with their inner child as if a near stranger inhabited them.

Minds are filled with words that presume to construct the inner, and not just the outer, world. Experts used to talk about "id" and "superego" almost as if these were tangible parts of a human being. Now they talk about dynamics and depressions, but with the same assumption of concreteness. Indeed, we have come to think, whether it's true or not, that we can feel, touch, massage, grab, or let go of pieces of our inner world.

This construct of our inner world, the stream of words we use to describe everything, the presumptions with which we engage both what is beyond us and inside us, might be called consciousness. At the core of consciousness, most people believe there is a "self" that holds everything together. Even those who feel that "self" is an illusion spend hours in an inner dialogue trying to trick their minds out of this common-sense assumption.

However we think of our inner mental world, whether it is primarily a stream of words or a succession of images, whether centered on the self or centered on getting rid of the self, whatever inner construct we have, God wants to be at the center.

What God asks of us, first of all, is that the world of our words be formed by the world of God's Word.

Revelation

It might seem somewhat strange to put this first commandment of discipleship this way: "You Shall Dwell in the Word of God." We don't normally think of dwelling in words, let alone in a word. But this commandment speaks to something basic about us and about God.

About us, the commandment alludes to the fact that we do make our world with images and words about them. The combination of image and word forms our individual and social world. We might wonder about how exactly this happens, whether consciousness is possible at all without using words, or whether we have already grasped something before the words help fix that picture in a particular way. Whichever way it works, it works.

Even if someone might argue that children do not live in a world of words (so maybe they don't have full human consciousness), who would deny that the first months of a baby's life are spent hearing the sounds out of which the baby's world will be formulated? The world over, in every culture, mothers and fathers are "gooing" and "ahhing" before their children's faces, providing them with the building blocks that will later become words. Almost from the start children mimic these sounds, practicing how to word things, until they have mastered language.

But this commandment also talks about how God addresses disciples, through the process believers call "revelation." One of the basic purposes of revelation is to be the way that God shapes the world of our words until a consciousness emerges. God's action and relationship with a people shaped a stream of language that is gathered in the Scriptures; these Scriptures shape the minds of believers. Through experiences and layers of verbal communication (spoken, sung, taught, memorized, eventually written), there came to be a collection of remarkable writings that, together, form a whole universe of disclosure. Whether those words were ancient legends, or family genealogies, or court records, or temple poems, or visions, or extended analogies, or wisdom sayings or parables, together they have created a way for God to be disclosed.

Of course there are many nonverbal parts to the process by which revelation shapes us. Much like the way we know something even before we can put it into words ("I have a hunch," or "It's on the tip of my tongue"), so believers find themselves involved in experiences so deep that images and subsequent words help them eventually to begin grasping the truth.

The first commandment, then, says that by submitting ourselves as disciples willing to listen, we want to learn how to bring the world of our own words into the world of God's Word. By hearing. By questioning. By absorbing. By sharing. And by dwelling.

The Bible

The Jewish people have given us perhaps the prime example of what it means to be a people who dwell in God's Word. The short quotation at the head of this chapter from the book of Deuteronomy to this day is posted by the doorway of every observant Jewish home. Called the "Shema Israel," this passage sums up how God's revelation should envelop the world of God's follower.

Precisely because there is only one God, and that God alone is Lord, the believer makes a place for God that nothing else occupies or competes with. Were God only one more item on a busy agenda, or one more theory to be tested, or one more nice image to enchant us, then God would not be God. By definition, God demands a central place in our lives. Human experience tells us that, until God does have this central place, God is, for all practical purposes, unknown. Indeed, we might use the word "God," but it has little real content. Throughout the book of Exodus, when Moses is trying to get Pharaoh to free the Egyptian people, the resounding verse, repeated again and again, is this: "Then you will know I am God" (e.g., Exod 6:7 and 7:5). In other words, because Pharaoh could not put aside his own world vision to make a place for God, God could not be known. And the consequences would be disastrous for him and his people.

Because God alone is God, God's Word alone has a place of absolute importance in our lives. As the book of Deuteronomy says, strap it on your forehead, sew it into the seam of your coat, recite it in the morning and the evening, tell your children and make them tell their children—because God's Word will accept no other words pretending to take its central place in human life.

How does God create this kind of mental environment? That is the primary task of God's Word, the Scriptures, which have their power only when they are read, only when written words become the living Word. Many homes, to be sure, have large Bibles in prominent places; unfortunately, most of those Bibles, if studies can be trusted, are largely unread, especially if they contain older, stilted translations without helpful notes.

If the Bible is to be read in order to come alive, modern disciples have today an advantage over disciples in virtually any other era of the Church's history. Modern disciples, first of all, can read the Bible in the context of the Church's biblical renewal that has, for virtually every mainline Christian church, developed a systematic way to read the Scriptures publicly at worship, weekend by weekend. The Scriptures no longer stand at the mercy of the favoritism of the preacher; rather, the Church leads its members through the main books and the major texts year by year. Believers, then, have the full panorama of the Scriptures laid out for them every three years. This has yet another advantage: In their personal reading, modern disciples can share common experience of God's Word being proclaimed out loud (which it was meant to be) and elaborated in the midst of a community of believers.

Secondly, modern disciples have a range of new, attractive, accurate, and annotated Scriptures to make reading easier. The result of archeology and language studies, these new translations make the Word of God more transparent and understandable than probably at any other time since they were written. The ancient texts are better edited and more accurate, with scholars today providing better notes and references to the various historical, cultural, and language factors behind the scriptural text.

Dwelling in the Scripture

In order for us to dwell in God's Word, to make the Word of God the basis of the words by which we understand ourselves, the disciples have to commit themselves to reading the Scriptures devoutly and regularly, both with their community of faith and personally. "If you continue in my word, you are truly my disciples," says Jesus (John 8:31), underscoring how the Word is an environment in which people stay.

Yet when it comes to the Word of God, most Christians seem to be very part-time renters, hardly dwellers at all. Some Christians, particularly Roman Catholics, do not even register the fact that half of their Sunday worship is devoted to proclaiming and understanding the Word of God. Again, with the exception of those Christians who call themselves "evangelical," only a small percentage of

Catholic and Protestant Christians read the Scriptures in their homes or in small groups with other believers.

Ignorance accounts for some of this; fear even more. The Scriptures, after all, make for a rather large book, with words and phrasings that seem highly unfamiliar when compared to daily patterns of speech. How does one begin to understand them? Even more of a deterrent is the truth that Christians seem to have been fighting over the some of the meaning of the Scriptures almost from the beginning. If after 2,000 years experts can argue about what a text means, where does that leave us? Yet another deterrent is that some Christians use the Bible as a weapon against others, even other believers, making them feel inadequate and irreligious. They do this by a confrontational approach, often based on a few memorized verses or select passages, which dismisses the religious experience of others. And yet another reason, maybe the most telling, is that the Scriptures make demands of those who read them, demands that people would prefer to avoid.

In spite of these deterrents, disciples today simply must read the Word of God or else they will not be able to "put on the mind of Christ," a mind that cannot be known without the Scriptures. Their reading must entail devotion, study, and wisdom.

- Devotion involves us in the Word such that we are swept into the consciousness of all things in God. It involves, among other things, feeling and attachment.
- Study frees us from misreadings and distortions of our understanding, while helping us relate God's Word to the rest of our knowledge.

- And wisdom helps us apply that Word to the concrete situations of our personal and social lives.

The Scriptures in Our Lives

For much of the Church's history, believers approached the Scriptures from four perspectives; they called these the "four senses" of the Scriptures. Today, disciples who want to make the Word of God central in their lives, can adapt these four perspectives as a way to help them appropriate the Scriptures in their personal and social lives.

Historical

The first perspective looks at the text and what it seems to be saying in terms of information, context, culture, and language. Another way to approach this is to ask: What is the literal meaning of the Scripture? But we must be careful here. The "literal meaning" hardly means we can read the Scriptures literally, as if, word for word, all biblical ideas could be directly translated into our contemporary ideas. In fact, we cannot do this even in modern languages because each language has its own context. In English we might talk about "discussing something." But if we use the word *discutir* in Spanish, the meaning is "arguing about something."

We cannot grasp the Scriptures if we are "literal minded." Rather, we can only grasp the historical and literal meaning of the text if we are willing to enter into the world of the ancient writers, those inspired by God, with the vocabulary, images, and ideas that were used in their times. After all, we can observe even across human generations that children speak and understand differently than adolescents or adults. Adolescents clearly use language differently than their parents. Words mean different things in different contexts.

The Scriptures invite us to leap into another world—the world of the ancient writers and witnesses—as a way of entering into the world of God's Word. The large array of current scriptural commentaries and annotated bibles can go a long way to providing this historical context for understanding the Scriptures.

Trying to grasp what was happening in the world of the biblical writer, and what it might mean for us, is one of the steps to making the Word of God the environment of our lives.

Analogical

For centuries, believers interpreted God's Word by asking how it compared to their lives and to other aspects of their faith. Even the earliest Christian writers describe how they came to view the Hebrew Scriptures through the particular lens of relating them to the events of Jesus' life (Luke 24:27). How do ancient stories about slavery and liberation teach us about our slavery and liberation in Jesus Christ? Or the new kinds of enslavement that even modern life brings? How do echoes of the Spirit's presence in the psalms expand into our more fully grasped presence of the Holy Spirit (e.g., Psa 51:11—"do not take your holy spirit from me")? Why has Psalm 110 been interpreted through Jesus the Messiah, virtually from the beginning of Christian writings (see the Letter to the Hebrews)?

The answer is in this analogical perspective: The Scriptures provide a meaning when compared to each other and to human experience. They ask to be related to our contemporary lives, both personally and socially. When I read a parable, do I see myself in it? What questions is that parable raising in my own life? What opportunities and what dangers is it outlining for the world in which we live? How do the Scriptures relate when our hearts are robust and daring; or when they are despairing and nearly broken?

Every Scriptural passage has the capacity to call us to renewal...because these passages speak to patterns in our lives that mirror biblical patterns. But this can happen only if we dwell in the Word, let it seep deeply into our own consciousness, shaping and molding until its mind is our own.

Moral

This perspective refers to the way the Scriptures invite us to get off our couches and do something. The Scriptures lead us to contemplation; and they inevitably, if we read them with sincerity, lead us to act. Saints throughout Christian history narrate how a passage here or there lead to a great breakthrough. This is a bit different than the method some people employ—when they have a problem, they close their eyes, open to a biblical passage randomly, and then construe that passage as some divine "Ann Landers" instruction about what to do. The Bible is not meant to be magic.

It is meant to convert us, to change the fundamental way we see and act, to hone our behavior until we become the mature disciples we are called to be. This hardly is magic. Rather, it is the work of God's Spirit. And it is discipline—a discipline that we can avail ourselves of every time we ask the Scriptures that we have read: How, then, should I live and how, then, must I change?

Eschatological

This strange word, which comes from the Greek word for "last thing," refers to the way the Scriptures point us forward on our pilgrim journeys. The Scriptures talk about the present, but they also guide us toward a future that begins in our present life but will find fulfillment only in eternal life. When we read the Scriptures, what are they telling us about hope, about the path we are called to take in the future, and about the home we eventually hope to have with the Lord and the saints?

Almost everyone has heard Robert Frost's famous poem about the two roads that diverged in the woods; the fame of this poem derives from the way it so perfectly reflects the paths of our own experience. We make choices that set us irretrievably down one road, and not another.

The Scriptures constantly invite us down new paths, some of them very much in line with our own dispositions, and some of them very much opposed to the easier road we might prefer. Continuing on the journey of faith is no easy thing, as we will explore in chapter seven—believers always face the temptation of bailing out and giving up.

The Scriptures also invite us to see how the paths we take, whether easy or difficult, terminate in a hoped-for kingdom where the promise of our existence will be fulfilled in God. Disciples, who recognize they travel down a pilgrim path, can see guideposts for their journey in the layers of meaning that come from the Scriptures. The final perspective for exploring the Scriptures is nothing else but the kingdom in its fullness.

In a world of specialization, when scientists and factory workers give their whole lives over to one specific study or one detailed procedure, every person has to ask what will form the framework of their minds and hearts.

The experience of millions of believers over thousands of years is that the Word of God, though encapsulated in the Bible, is vast and broad. It encompasses all creation and speaks to every layer of the heart.

It is, to use a popular image, "a big tent," where we, individually and as a human community, can easily dwell.

Questions for Reflection

What seem to be the ways that modern people understand themselves and make sense of their lives? What would you say are the central images by which people live today? What are the adequacies and limitations of these images?

What role have the Scriptures played in your life and the life of your faith community? In what ways have the Scriptures become familiar? In what ways do the Scriptures still seem inaccessible? What can make the Scriptures more "user friendly"?

What are the ways you mostly make sense of the Scriptures? In what ways do you recognize the four traditional perspectives (historical, analogical, moral, eschatological) in your own reflection on the Scriptures? What is the level of biblical understanding and expression in your faith community?

What ways can you think of to deepen your own sense of the Scriptures? What would help deepen them in your local congregation? How can the Bible be read more often and better?

How would you comment on St. Jerome's statement: "To be ignorant of the Scriptures is to be ignorant of Christ"?

[Each chapter will suggest some practices that disciples can cultivate to deepen their following of Jesus, and also some further scripture reading to explore. These suggestions and passages obviously are

meant to be pursued over time as a way to develop our Christian maturity. "Developing our Discipleship" and "Exploring the Scriptures" present long-term tasks to help shape our discipleship.]

Developing Our Discipleship

Choose at least one of the following as a disciplined response to the first commandment of discipleship, dwelling in God's Word:

- Commit to read and pray over the Scriptures every day for at least 15 minutes.
- Commit to studying at least one book of the Bible each year, using notes and commentaries.
- Commit to sharing with others using the Scriptures on a regular basis. Consider the following:
  - spouse or family
  - small discussion group from church
  - small group developed in the workplace
  - ministry group from church or neighborhood
  - neighbors who wish to explore the Scriptures.
- Commit to finding ways to get sound answers to questions that arise from Scripture reading from people who are competent and trained.

CAUTION

When you undertake to make God's Word the center of your life, using the sacred Scriptures, make sure that you provide a healthy environment to accomplish this. Some people want to share Scriptures, but they may have an angle and an axe to grind because they primarily seek to win members (even from among other believers) for their own denominations, or to dismiss the faith of some believers on the basis of caricatures.

If studying the Scriptures starts making someone uneasy, that person should ask where the unease is coming from. The Scriptures will surely challenge us and the way we live; but that is different from the possible efforts of some people to move us away from sound faith on the basis of their own preferences or prejudices.

Reading Scriptures presumes a context. One of the oldest arguments in Western Christianity concerns whether an individual's interpretation of the Scriptures is the major reference point, or whether the community of faith is the major reference point. However Christians think about this debate, they should recognize that the way the question is posed is not helpful. We always read the Scriptures with reference to our various communities—church, family, friends, culture, and so on. We never read the Scriptures "alone" because the language we use to interpret the Scriptures comes from others. To read the Scriptures ignoring the insights of two thousand years of other believers' understanding would certainly be arrogant. At the same time, every community of faith knows that individuals must personally deal with the impact of the Scriptures on their lives.

Exploring the Scriptures

Read the story of the Jewish escape from Egypt in the book of Exodus; notice how important recognizing God is to the movement of the story (Exod 1—15).

Read the great passages of consolation that begin with the sixtieth chapter of Isaiah; experience the sweep of the language and imagery that this prophet gives us.

Read the Sermon on the Mount (Matthew 5—7) as if you were actually listening to Jesus; try to hear his word and passion in a fresh way.

Mapping the Disciple's Path

God would enter the inner world of our consciousness.

Revelation, through our attending to the Scriptures, is how God shapes our world.

To let God shape our world, we must let God be first, with nothing else taking God's place.

Through devotion, study, and applying the Scriptures in our lives, we take on the disciple's mind.

Letting God shape our world leads us to:

Worshipping God with all we are.

Chapter Two

You Shall Worship the Lord Your God

So what does God ask of us?

> I appeal to you therefore, brothers and sisters, by the mercies of God, to present your bodies as a living sacrifice, holy and acceptable to God, which is your spiritual worship. (Rom 12:1)

A composer wakes up with a new strain of music beginning somewhere within, so deep inside that he cannot even locate it. He gives himself to the strain, the flow, the rhythm, the possible directions. When it has ripened enough inside of him, it has to be expressed. It comes forth as a song or melody, expressed on paper and, best of all, through voice and musical instruments.

A father thinks of his daughter during work, a smile arising immediately on his face. What will she be doing when he arrives home? What will her mood be? What will she say about her mother, her day, her friends? How will she greet her father? Before arriving home, the father stops to buy a little gift. He has to express his love.

The scientist has considered a problem from many angles. She's reviewed the various studies, run experiments herself, put the question in multiple forms, talked it over with her students and confreres. Sitting at her desk, reviewing the data once more, she finds a new idea emerging from her reflections. She sketches its main points as simply as she can and then, over the next week or two, matches those points with the data again and again. Can it be? Yes, she has indeed discovered a new way to approach the problem. She cannot wait to write it down, to explain it, because it cannot stay only in her mind.

Any powerful consciousness or conviction, almost by its very power, forces itself to be expressed. When it is expressed, that powerful consciousness is confirmed and others have a chance to share in it.

The melody in one's mind becomes the tune on the radio. The smile on a father's face becomes the shared joy of father and daughter greeting each other. The scientist's breakthrough becomes the understanding of all who read her published paper and duplicate her experiments.

Of course we might argue that a million ideas have never been published, a million sighs have never been requited, and myriads of melodies have disappeared from musicians' minds as quickly as they began. All true. But if they had any cogency or vitality, whatever happened as a result, they surely were moving toward expression. Expression is perhaps part of the conviction itself because our imagination is never entirely private. When we talk to ourselves, it's as if we are talking with another, as if we are expressing our mind.

Prayer

We've all heard definitions of prayer, and most of us probably can stammer to something like: "Prayer is lifting our hearts and minds toward God." We also know by our experience that prayer is not fully grasped by definitions; it is best known in its exercise. Prayer, after all, is an action word, a verb—lifting hearts, crying out, praising, even groaning (Rom 8:26).

Because of prayer's dynamic quality, perhaps at this point we can be satisfied by a working description of prayer: Prayer is the expression of our relationship with God. Just as any powerful conviction or any new insight surges forth into some kind of expression, so when a person has a relationship with God, with God as the center of life, that person must somehow express this realization.

This working description simplifies our attempts to categorize prayer because our own experience shows us that prayer is sometimes quiet and reflective, sometimes labored and mechanical, sometimes exploding in song, sometimes rapid in feeling, sometimes ritualized, and sometimes so spontaneous that we have no idea where it came from. But whatever form prayer takes, all these actions of prayer express aspects of our relationship with God, with God as the center of our consciousness.

So the Word of God, in which we are to dwell, by its power in us moves us to expression, to prayer. Can we hear the Scripture without it echoing inside of us, starting some kind of chatter within, and quickly taking expression by the movement of our lips or the racing of our thoughts? The great Christian religious teachers who developed systems of meditation merely elaborated this process into a method that others could follow—from Scripture, to image, to involvement in the image, to response to that involvement, to expression in prayer.

Even a kind of prayer that seems so personal like centering prayer, in which one tries not to form ideas or say words, is also an expression of our relationship with God. Rather than words or music being the expression, the one praying becomes an expression, in his or her very being, of a consciousness of God. The sitting still, the attending, the willingness to be totally opened, the gentle brushing away of any content coming to the mind or any urge coming to the will, all serves the purpose of simply dwelling before the divine.

Surveys of modern believers show almost everyone prays at least in some rudimentary way. Indeed, they would have to because it would be almost a contradiction to say one believed in God—as almost everyone says—and then not express that belief somehow. But just as our consciousness of God can be very low, because we do not dwell deeply in God's Word, so our expressing our relationship with God can be rather incidental in life: a fleeting thought in the morning, a head-bowing gesture near a church, a quickly recited prayer at a moment of stress, a perfunctory thank-you-God before drifting off to sleep.

The disciple, though, does not have perfunctory relationship with God, a fleeting encounter with God's Word. The disciple, dwelling in God's Word, lets God take over a life—mind and mentality, spirit and spirituality, desires and morality, hopes and life project. For a disciple, merely nodding at God in some perfunctory way betrays the experience of God. The disciple must make prayer central to his or her life because God has become central, crucial, to the disciple's life.

The Root and Flower of Prayer

Long-time Christian thought has identified four kinds of prayer: 1) adoration and 2) thanksgiving, which responds joyfully to what God has given to us; 3) petition, and 4) intercession for another, which bring our needs, often in pain, before God. Clearly these four kinds of prayer reflect two fundamental directions that prayer can take—when our hearts seem empty, and when they are overflowing. These two directions of prayer represent the flowering of a single root—the central mystery of Christian faith, the death and resurrection of Jesus.

Putting on the mind of Christ (Phil 2:5)—what it means to dwell in his Word—has to involve our dealing with the central act of Jesus' life, his death and resurrection. For the drama of dying and rising constitutes the pattern of Christian life just as it was the kernel of Christ's own life—the Paschal Mystery which Christians celebrate and proclaim during Holy Week. Following Jesus means dying and rising in him, taking up his cross in the crosses of our own daily existence (Matt 16:24).

St. Paul saw this pattern in much of the Christian's life, but especially in the sacrament of baptism. He writes to the Romans:

> Do you not know that all of us who have been baptized into Christ Jesus were baptized into his death? Therefore we have been buried with him by baptism into death, so that, just as Christ was raised from the dead by the glory of the Father, so we too might walk in newness of life. For if we have been united with him in a death like his, we will certainly be united with him in a resurrection like his. (6:3ff.)

St. Paul meant this pattern to be more than one convenient image. Rather, in the drama of a disciple's existence one will find participation in the death and life of Jesus Christ—spiritually, sacramentally in worship, and morally in the values of one's daily life. That's why, in the citation at the beginning of this chapter, Paul could urge that believers make *their very selves* into sacrifices of praise because he saw Jesus' sacrificial love as an act of praise and glory. St. John also sees the same pattern because once Judas leaves the upper chamber to betray Jesus, Jesus immediately begins to speak about how he will be glorified—in his dying and rising—and how that glory will be revealed in the love that Christians have for each other (13:30–35). John shows us the same linking of spirituality, worship, and moral life.

Do not the death and resurrection of Jesus parallel the two directions of prayer, petition and adoration, the need for life and overflowing life? Are not the most powerful words of petition spoken, in the Gospels, by the dying Jesus? "My God, my God, why have you forsaken me? [Matt 27:46]....Father, into your hands I commend my spirit [Luke 23:46]....Father, forgive them; for they do not know what they are doing [Luke 23:34]." In these and similar words of Jesus in his agony, we feel the inner substance of Jesus reaching out in need to the Father.

Yet the rising of Jesus from the dead, the unexpected and unpredictable response of the Father to Jesus' pleas, leads to nothing less than adoration, the awestruck beholding of Jesus' in his risen glory, and the unrestrained praise of God for raising Jesus from the dead. "[T]he disciples rejoiced when they saw the Lord [John 20:20]....Thomas answered him, 'My Lord and my God!' [John 20:28]....When they saw him, they worshipped him; but some doubted [Matt 28:17]."

The root of prayer, the experience of Jesus' death and resurrection that believers have as their own experience through the Holy Spirit, flowers into the two fundamental dimensions of prayer. But each of these dimensions of prayer, when reflected on, come to the same act of standing outside ourselves, either from need or from awe, in a desire to give ourselves completely to God.

When we truly need, we are pulled beyond ourselves.

When we truly exalt, we are drawn beyond ourselves.

In each case, prayer brings us in total trust before the being of God, stripped of all pretensions and selfishness. We stand on the edge of our existence, humbled and thrilled by the vastness of the divine beyond us and, in a real way, within us. Mystics have this experience of "ecstasy" (=standing on the edge) with frequency; however, most believers experience some states of transport during their faith life.

We stand with Jesus Christ on the cross, hovering between death and hope; we stand with him on life's horizon, lifted into God's power so he can bestow the Spirit of power on the world.

When the disciple prays, expressing the deepest relationship with God, the disciple experiences the Paschal Mystery of Jesus and partakes of the Spirit Jesus sends. Praying most deeply, the disciple comes closest to the mind of Christ.

How can it happen that the experience of a Prophet two millennia ago has effect even now? How can it be that our contemporary lives mesh with the biography of One attested to in the ancient Gospels? Only the believers' experiences of the Spirit of God show how this is possible, from the first breathing upon the disciples that Jesus did after his resurrection (John 20:22) to the powerful personal-and-communal experience of the Spirit as the outpouring of God's unrestrained gift upon the disciples (Acts 2:1–10).

The Christian cannot identify with Jesus Christ except through the Spirit's work in his or her life; this work happens in the Christian's experience. The earliest followers of Jesus, struggling to make sense of his death, and learning how to proclaim his resurrection, were overwhelmed to experience the Spirit acting in their lives (see Acts 8:15–17; 10:44–45). Christians express their identification with Jesus through their teaching about the Trinity: Jesus brings us into relationship with God, his Father, through his dying and rising; he does this through the bestowal of his Spirit. To grasp the mind of Jesus is to understand God as Trinity, one infinite being relating to us in the three persons of Father, Son, and Spirit.

Personal and Communal

When disciples stand outside themselves in complete trust of God, in adoration and in need, they do this both personally and as part of a community of faith.

The ways of personal prayer take many forms. Indeed, the history of Christian life, from the first outlines of worship that came from Jewish sources, through the development of monasticism in the Eastern and Western churches, to the emergence of pious societies that emphasized personal devotion to Jesus Christ, to the foundation of religious orders to emphasize particular gifts like preaching or poverty, to the insights of the Protestant Reformers and the influences they have continued to generate, to the revival movements across all forms of Christianity, to the twentieth century's development of an ecumenical spirituality and the meeting of world bishops at the Vatican in the 1960s—this history demonstrates the breadth of spiritual options open to a disciple.

This diversity of expressions of personal prayer invites the individual disciple to discover the kind of personal praying that will lead to prayer's goal: expressing our relationship with God through the process of dying and rising, brought about by the Holy Spirit.

Saints such as Francis de Sales, when he wrote his *Introduction to the Devout Life* in Geneva in the seventeenth century, argued that each way of life called for a distinct form of holiness. This insight also applies to one's life of prayer.

Although common sources of praying, such as the Psalms or the words of biblical prophets or the Gospels themselves, have to be the bread-and-butter of every disciple, other sources of prayer have to develop from each particular way of life. Not everyone can spend an hour in meditation every day; particular prayer forms, such as centering prayer or the Rosary, might not seem suitable for certain kinds of personalities.

One will notice, too, as one goes through life that different prayer forms take on different meaning. Youth might find a lot of detail and energy in meditation; with time, however, meditation might become wordless and almost formless. Reading a psalm word by word might lead one to deeper prayer at one point in life; at another, just recalling the heart of a psalm might be more effective. The ability to concentrate diminishes at points in one's life—how many elderly people, with their prescriptions and mental changes, complain that "they cannot pray anymore" when perhaps they are doing the most effective prayer of their lives? Our callings, our personal gifts, and the various stages of our development all play on the kind of prayer that makes sense in an individual's life.

There seem to be, however, two foundations to personal prayer: 1) a constant return to the various parts of Scripture as part of our personal meditation and discussion; and 2) a testing of prayer's effectiveness by the way it brings a disciple more deeply into ongoing conversion, that is, the capacity to die and rise in Christ. For every disciple will experience transitions on the pilgrim's journey. In these transitions, the baggage of resentments, vices, and selfishness, shows itself again in new says. What one thought was conquered often returns in a new guise. The invitation to "take up the cross" applies directly to these moments, when God invites us to move beyond our present stage, into a deeper relationship, by experiencing death and resurrection in our personal spirituality.

These may well be the most difficult moments in a disciple's life, for we all are tempted to smugness and inertia. The work of the Holy Spirit in us, through personal prayer, supported by spiritual counsel with those one trusts, and the broader experience of the church in prayer, brings about just such personal renewal when we dare to plumb deeper in relationship to God.

Christians have found models of prayer in others. Certain outstanding expressions of holiness fascinate believers—whether monks, reformers, servants of the poor, mystics, or those who marvelously show the holiness of everyday life. Certain images from the Scriptures likewise can be models of personal prayer—one thinks of John the Baptist, Paul, Mary Magdalene, John the Evangelist, Peter and, if Christian history is a guide, the sweeping influence of Mary, the mother of Jesus. These followers of Jesus become something like icons in the life of believers. Entering into the angles of spiritual growth that these figures represent can dramatically expand a person's spiritual life.

When we are led to plumb ever-deeper relationships with God, in the pattern of the dying and rising of Jesus, our prayer life will contain dimensions that spiritual writers have often seen in Christian life: purification, illumination, and union. In other words, we continue to die to ourselves, we continue to have insight into ourselves as we put on the mind of Christ, and we continue to experience periods of intense unity with God. These dimensions do not come in sequence, to be sure. Periods of great consolation may be followed by periods of great testing. Yet the disciple, in personal prayer, who is graced with moments in which his or her being seems in accord with God's, receives a strength that can make the hardest points of the journey easier to take. These moments of something like ecstasy intimate for the believer the ultimate goal of human life.

Yet because discipleship is not a solitary following of Jesus, but a walking after him in community with others, prayer is not just solitary. We pray alone, but we also pray in union with others, expressing the needs and the praise of all humanity, indeed of all creation. In us, existence itself reaches its edge and, through prayer, transcends itself in God.

Disciples commit themselves to pray alone; they also commit themselves to pray together with other believers. Both kinds of prayer run through the Christian Scriptures, from the example of Jesus spending nights alone in prayer (Luke 6:12; 21:37), to the adoration the apostles gave to the Lord before and after his death (Matt 28:17, Luke 24:51–52). Acts frequently shows believers coming together for prayer in community (Acts 2:41–47; 4:31–32). The final book of the Bible, Revelation, so notoriously difficult to interpret, shows scene after scene of adoration and praise on the part of the redeemed, reflecting the kind of worship that was part of the ritual in Asia Minor (see, e.g., Rev 5:9ff.; 7:10ff.; 11:16ff.; 15:3ff.; 19:1ff.).

The personal and communal nature of prayer converges in the use that believers make of the Book of Psalms. These ancient hymns of Israel have become the steady expression of both our individual and collective relationship with God. Psalms fill the worship of the Eastern Orthodox and the Western Catholic churches. They form the background of daily worship in the major Protestant denominations; they also provide the imagery for the prayer and song of evangelical Protestant communions.

Every believer could well make the Psalms his or her own prayer. The range of feeling, the swing from plea to exaltation, the trusting abandon, the spiritual depth, speak to both our personal experience and that of our faith community as well. St. Augustine saw the Psalms as the cry of Christ—both as head, in himself, and as body, in his people. To sit quietly with a psalm and let the words seep into us, draw us from ourselves, push us to the limit of our feeling, and invite us beyond all that through giving ourselves to God in love—this is to experience humankind in relationship with its Creator and Savior.

Personal prayer needs communal prayer to keep it from becoming simply talking-to-ourselves. Communal prayer needs personal prayer to keep it from being simply recited words. Every disciple must work hard to appropriate the community's worship deep inside the heart; and every community must work hard to pull the hearts of its members together in joined prayer.

Perhaps nothing expresses the communal nature of prayer more than those actions that are called the sacraments, notably baptism and Eucharist (The Lord's Supper), along with the other major sacred rites. In these actions, our deepest needs blend seamlessly with our greatest desires to praise God. The ritual of washing and eating dramatizes the redemption of the whole person, body and spirit. The union for which prayer strives—to touch God in love—comes about in the mystery of the shared Body and Blood of Jesus. Every other ritual gesture, every other sacrament, finds its meaning in relation to the sacred meal when Jesus invites us to his table, sits with us in love, and gives himself as nourishment for the pilgrim.

When, in the early thirteenth century, young Francis gave up his inheritance and his wardrobe in Assisi about eight hundred years ago, he spent much time in prayer by himself on the outskirts of town. During one of those periods of prayer, he heard a crucifix speak. "Rebuild my church," he heard Jesus say. After repairing some abandoned churches, he realized the voice's meaning more clearly. Jesus wanted him to build up the community of believers.

If the Word of God abides in us, and we dwell in that Word ourselves, we are led to prayer as individuals and as a community of faith. God's commandment calls us to look within our hearts and within the heart of our human family. Whatever else we think is important, worth our effort and needing our sacrifice, it is God alone that we are to worship. For only in worship do we express what is central to our lives—and all existence—our relationship with God.

Questions for Reflection

What are the popular and powerful forms of expression that seem to populate modern life? What do these tell us about creativity? Why do these seem to draw people together?

What is your sense of the phrase "relationship with God"? How does God become manifest, living, vital to you? In what ways can you describe your prayer, in its various forms, as expressing your relationship with God?

What have been the most powerful moments of prayer for you? In what ways did they express your need? In what ways did they express the overflowing abundance of grace?

Reflect on the relationship of personal and communal prayer. Describe the particular ways that one reinforces the other. Can you think of ways in which they can reinforce each other more powerfully in today's church?

Developing Our Discipleship

Because prayer is the expressing of our relation with God, disciples do not have a choice of whether to pray or not. Without prayer the relationship is dead. Only fools deceive themselves by saying that they have faith...and then think they can absolve themselves of a life of prayer. Can I say I'm alive but refuse my heart to beat, my lungs to breathe, my mind to think?

Disciples commit themselves to:

Daily Prayer

– Marking the hours of the day, morning and evening, with prayer.
– Spending quiet time each day listening to God and expressing what is in our hearts to God.

This daily prayer can be done alone or, preferably at times, with others, particularly families or friends. It can be characterized by biblical prayer and Scripture, or by devotional prayer such as meditation or the rosary (which itself involves a lot of meditation).

Many priests and religious, and a growing number of lay people, commit themselves to praying the Liturgy of the Hours, *the Church's official method of prayer to sanctify human time by scriptural prayer.*

Sunday Prayer

– Making the Day of Christ's Resurrection revolve around the community's worship through the Eucharist.
– Creating a real Sabbath of rest and reflection on the Lord's Day.
– Making the scriptural selections of the Sunday Eucharist and the prayers points of meditation and personal reflection before and after Sunday worship.

Exploring the Scriptures

Read the elaborate directions for the setting up of the tent of worship in the book of Exodus (chapter 26ff.). Try to get a flavor for the place of communal worship for these ancient believers.

Read the sixth chapter of John's Gospel and reflect on the depth and variety of imagery given to the Eucharist, the bread that is the body of Christ.

Explore the fourteenth Chapter of 1 Corinthians to see the difficulties with worship in this early Christian community. Read on to the fifteenth chapter to see how Paul develops the place, and decorum, of the Eucharist for the Corinthians.

Mapping the Disciple's Path

A powerful awareness inevitably leads to expression.

Prayer is the expression of our relationship with God,
the central relationship of our lives.

Prayer draws us beyond ourselves in adoration and petition.

This happens in parallel to the dying and rising of Jesus,
which the Spirit accomplishes in us,
bringing us to Christ's experience of God.

In the experience of the God of Jesus, the Trinity,
we pray personally and as a community.

Prayer so changes our lives that we come to:

Live in fidelity to God and God's Word.

Chapter Three

You Shall Live in Fidelity to the Word of God

So what does God expect of us?

Be perfect, therefore, as your heavenly Father is perfect. (Matt 5:48)

Mirrors only help a little. Human experience is made all the stranger because the one thing we notice about everyone else, the face, is the one thing hardest to see in ourselves. Of course we have the ancient myth of Narcissus that tells the story of the young god who, seeing himself in the water, falls in love with his own image; because that image disappeared every time Narcissus would try to grasp it, he died heartbroken for his own face. But a mirror might have been worse than water.

Mirrors, after all, give us the impression that we can see our faces the way we see the faces of others. They make part of what Narcissus tried to do easier—seeing oneself. But this very ease only shows the other part of his dilemma: We can no more grasp our faces than this ancient god could grasp his face. We only think we can.

Staring in mirrors, we can isolate our focus on different parts of our face, look at our hair or our eyebrows, or our lips. But this kind of seeing is itself a distortion because, unlike our perception of the faces of others, we can never take in the whole face . We get only pieces, exaggerated, out of perspective, out of kilter.

We have a hard time seeing our own faces; we probably have a harder time looking into our own inner selves. We often have been given the impression that, like a mirror, we can look at the inside of ourselves. Yet grasping ourselves, like grasping our own faces, seems forever elusive. We get pieces, but we get them disjointed, concentrating here and there on a feeling, an attitude, a habit, a thought. But when we close in on any of those mental states or actions, they seem to change just as we are about to grasp them. What was really behind that burst of anger? When we think we have that in hand, something else occurs to us, depending on any number of moods. Like Hiesenberg's uncertainly principle in physics, which defined limits on human observation of atomic particles, our very observation changes what we thought was there to see.

Is there some better mirror for the depths of our spirits?

The Letter of James has a rather obscure reference to mirrors. James is talking about the difficulty of conversion, of personal change. "For if any are hearers of the word and not doers, they are like those who look at themselves in a mirror; for they look at themselves and, on going away, immediately forget what they were like. But those who look into the perfect law, the law of liberty, and persevere, being not hearers who forget but doers who act—they will be blessed in their doing" (Jas 1:23–25).

James's metaphor seems obscure because most of us imagine we remember how we look, having looked in mirrors many times. It's only when he applies this image to the problem of doing, as opposed to hearing or saying, that the point of his image comes into focus. We see but we don't get it. We hear but we don't do it. We think we see, but we really are blind. Only by comparing our actions to a real ideal, a set of values outside ourselves, only then can we get a true picture of who we are.

Of course, James is dead right when he implies that seeing is deceptive. So often we fall for pretty faces, imputing onto them all kinds of nice attributes without any reason at all. Modern entertainment thrives on our need to read into faces a range of positive or attractive qualities. This alone explains why actors, actresses, sports heroes, and the like receive many media platforms to pronounce on a whole range of issues—and their word is taken as a kind of gospel. Our local pastors or bishops simply do not get that kind of credibility unless, by chance, they happen to have pretty faces too.

Because we never see our faces accurately, we naturally often presume we have pretty faces, or faces at least pretty enough to allow us to pronounce over our own lives, avoiding our obvious faults and presuming the best intentions of ourselves, in spite of the evidence. The way we let pretty faces lead us along, we also let the pretty talk in own heads string us along concerning our own lives. Even if most of us doubt our charm or beauty, we still mostly fall for the pretty lines in our own heads by which we constantly seduce ourselves.

It's only when we have to match ourselves to ideals and values that are outside ourselves that our true qualities begin to be revealed. James call this the "perfect law, the law of liberty." He seems to mean the rule of God that espouses ideals which conform to our most authentic needs. The rule of God that sets us free. The rule of God that brings us to our true selves. Seeing that law, and living it, means that our most beautiful image has a chance to emerge—when we come to reflect the qualities of God in our own lives.

Living God's Word

If we dwell in the Word of God, and make God the center of our lives through prayer, then our inner selves are filled with ideals, ideas, and images that come to bear upon our lives. We have seen how these images can become ways to understand the most profound drama of ourselves, particularly through the pattern of dying and rising. The notion of holiness, of perfection, is another way to think about this, but not an easy one.

The difficulty comes from the way cultures have overlaid veneers that can distort the basic idea of holiness. It is clear, for example, that a good part of the ancient Hebrew view of holiness revolved around issues of sanitation and behavioral codes that arose from that culture. What one could eat, how one should dress, how to resolve disputes, and what one could or could not do prior to worship, were all colored by the culture of that period.

In more recent centuries, holiness and purity received a very monastic and virginal coating, seeming to exclude almost everyone except those few who managed to live virginal purity. Even if we look for a less stringent ideal of holiness, we still often veer to the heroic or the exceptional. And that, in itself, leaves out most believers. Holiness was the mystic in a monastic cell, the youth never bothered by "impure thoughts," the rich person who renounced all wealth to serve the poor, but not the average man or woman who has to navigate the numerous adjustments that daily life calls for.

How do we reconcile these more heroic notions of holiness with the fact that all who are baptized receive a calling to be holy? When God asks us to be holy, what is God asking of us? What can this mean?

When the Word of God becomes the basis of life, then only one ideal, one passion, makes sense for the believer: to reflect the being of God in human existence, to live the Word of God in and through our own actions. In fact, the Christian Scriptures are quite consistent about this. Matthew's Sermon on the Mount, Luke's Sermon on the Plain, and John's new law of love (perhaps like James's law of liberty), all make the same argument: God must be reflected in our lives, our actions and qualities mirroring God's, if we would be children of God and inheritors of the kingdom.

So this third commandment of discipleship, living in fidelity to God's Word, emerges from the first two: Having dwelt in God's Word, having expressed our relationship with God in worship, how does a disciple consistently reflect and faithfully live out that Word? By *living in* the kingdom, *living for* the kingdom, and *living without* those things the kingdom insists we reject.

Living in the Kingdom: The Qualities of God

Fidelity to God's Word means, first of all, a "living in" the kingdom and the relationships that the kingdom calls us to have. Fidelity to the Word of God entails echoing in ourselves what we believe about God. The citation that begins this chapter certainly is intimidating: "Be perfect, therefore, as your heavenly Father is perfect" (Matt 5:48). This comes from the Sermon on the Mount where Jesus lays out the spiritual blueprint for his disciples. He calls them to live with a holiness that exceeds that of the greatest religious practitioners of his day—the Pharisees and Scribes (Matt 5:20), who were extremely devout and explicit lovers of God. Jesus wants more from his disciples.

He expects them to be perfect. How so? If we understand perfection to be a kind of omnipotence or a power to create from nothing, then living God's perfection would obviously be impossible. None of us can be like God in this sense.

So what does Jesus mean by this? The sense of "perfection" here is something like what an artist feels when he has completed a work, or a designer might experience when she has finished a line of clothing. There is a "finished" quality, something polished and complete. Being "perfect," or being "finished" or "complete," means that our discipleship, our learning, has enabled us to incorporate into our behaviors, over time, the qualities that we mostly attribute to God. These qualities instilled in our lives, despite our tendency toward sin and personal faults, prove that we have listened to God's Word enough, dwelled in it, so that God is mirrored in our own lives. They give evidence that we are children of God (Matt 5:45).

Jesus argues that God is generous, letting rain fall on the just and unjust (Matt 5:45); that God is merciful (Matt 18:33; Luke 6:36), even anticipating forgiveness for those who turn back (Luke 15:20). Peter realizes that God shows no partiality; everyone has access to God (Acts 10:34). John affirms that God is love; only by reflecting that love in our lives can we be truly children of God (John 13:34; 1 John 4:16). St. John's tradition also affirms that every follower of God is pure in the sense of complete integrity of self (and not just in a sexual way), even as God is pure (1 John 3:3).

Fidelity to God calls for a vigorous examination of our lives, with God as the model of our action, particularly as God has been revealed in Jesus Christ. "Just as I have loved you, you also should love one another" (John 13:34).

A moral life obsessed with faults and sins starts at the wrong place. A moral life that starts with God, and asks the Spirit of God to shape it to conform to God, is beginning to get the point of what Gospel fidelity is about.

Living for the Kingdom: Generosity and the Problem of Concupiscence

Yet another dimension of faithfulness to God involves a "living for"—making the kingdom the center of our lives, and not ourselves. Fidelity has to confront the problem of egocentricity that besets human nature.

However we understand the legacy of our first parents, Adam and Eve, who stand at the beginning of our stock as exemplars of what would come forth from us, the place of self-centeredness and preoccupation has to be near the top of that legacy. The great ancient Fathers who wrote about human nature used the word *concupiscence* to describe how we have a built-in tendency to refer everything to ourselves, to see ourselves at the center of our world.

Perhaps this paradoxically comes not from how sure we feel about ourselves, but from how empty we sense ourselves to be, how frail and vulnerable we feel. Like some cornered animal frightened for its existence, we inflate ourselves, hoping to look good even though we are filled with feelings of inadequacy. How often do modern people describe behaviors that hide their profound self-preoccupation and self doubt? "I was feeling bad, so I went out to the mall and brought myself something nice." "Whenever I feel down, I go get a nice steak dinner with cheesecake for desert. It makes me feel much better." Self-absorption does not necessarily arise from pride; self-centeredness easily arises from feelings of emptiness.

Often "concupiscence" has been understood almost exclusively in sexual terms. We instinctively think of the tendencies of the "flesh" toward lust as the basic battleground for grace and goodness. And certainly our sexual integrity is a crucial issue for our discipleship; indeed, so irresponsible have people become sexually according to the "normlessness" of today's world, it is crucial for the well-being of society itself. Only a culture as oversexed as ours, bewitched by empty fantasies of psychological wholeness tied to our sexual self-images, can commit the evil that it does in the name of love, with the debris of broken lives, twisted relationships, and aborted children in its wake.

But sexuality is only one field in which concupiscence plays out itself. It shows, in perhaps a more dramatic way, what happens more subtly in so much else of our lives—our greed, our self-assertion at the expense of others, our drive for power, our rage at a world that just doesn't come up to our specifications, our smallness of heart.

Discipleship confronts this egocentricity by begetting in us the same generosity of spirit that God shows. As part of following Jesus, disciples have to be instilled with the trust that Jesus calls them to have—a trust so great, we can forget about ourselves. The choice comes down to either living our lives with trust in God because God's generosity is so transparent; or living our insecure lives without trust—and missing most of the gifts that God constantly pours into our lives. In our popular thinking, it's often the millionaires who have the hardest time seeing all they have. Our culture loves to sing (but has a difficult time living), "The best things in life are free."

Living for the kingdom brings us to the endless fountain of generosity that surges in the core of our existence. How will we live in the face of that? "If you then, who are evil, know how to give good gifts to your children, how much more will your Father in heaven give good things to those who ask him!" (Matt 7:11) To the extent that we are self-centered, and unfree to live for others, to that extent we do not know the mind of Jesus Christ.

Living Without: What the Kingdom Asks Us to Give Up

If we take "living in" and "living for" seriously, then we must also decide what we can and must "live without." The disciple, to be faithful to God, must tear from his or her life whatever does not belong there because it does not conform to God. The disciple must set his or her face away from sin.

The aversion to sin ranks among the constant messages of the Scriptures, and the refinement of what sin means grows with the development of revelation. The legal expression of sin in the earlier books of the Hebrew Scriptures, where sin is measured as failure to live in accord with the law of God (which included cultic law), must be read alongside the insights of the prophets, who saw sin as a failure of relationship, both personal and corporate, with God. Hosea uses love-talk to express the complexity of this relationship (see, for example, Hosea 2:4, 11:4, 12:6, and 14:4). Isaiah's sweeping poetry, Jeremiah's personal struggles, and Ezekiel's prophetic actions all reveal something greater than just keeping the law. "...For the word of the LORD has become for me a reproach and derision all day long. If I say, 'I will not mention him, or speak any more in his name,' then within me there is something like a burning fire shut up in my bones; I am weary with holding it in, and I cannot" (Jer 20:8–9). With the prophets we are well beyond a required fulfilling of obligations. The obligations they felt arose from their relationship, intense and inescapable, with God.

Sin is what happens when God no longer is the center of our lives, and we no longer express God's centrality in our actions. It is the way our deeds dramatically testify that God's values are not our own. The Wisdom writers saw the law as a way of life and thought, a discipline to guide us. "I have taught you the way of wisdom; I have led you in the paths of uprightness. When you walk, your step will not be hampered; and if you run, you will not stumble. Keep hold of instruction; do not let go, guard her, for she is your life. Do not enter the path of the wicked, and do not walk in the way of evildoers" (Prov 4:11–14). Sin diverts us from this way of life, leading us to ruin.

Jesus builds upon all these senses of the Hebrew Scriptures, calling on his disciples to renounce not only the exterior actions of sin, but even the inner dispositions that lead to sin. Without calling us to the scrupulosity that some Christians have erected on Jesus' words, Jesus still demands that our impulses toward lust, greed, and anger be as ruthlessly renounced as the actions which they can lead to. (See Matt 5:21–43 for the ways Jesus develops these ideas in the Sermon on the Mount.)

Christian history has created many split worlds that somehow do not always seem to hang together. So Christians sometimes (and erroneously) speak of faith and reason, this world and the next, nature and supernature, human works and grace as if all of these dualities were opposites and enemies of each other. The result has often been a Christian life suspended between two unacceptable extremes. How many times have people seemed forced to choose between "God's Word" and "mere human reason"? As if the God who created in Truth could not bear our quest for truth. Because he saw religion seducing people to suffer through all kinds of indignities and injustices for the sake of some kingdom yet to come, Karl Marx criticized religion as the "opiate of the people." As if the kingdom to come did not have its start in our own world into which Jesus came. Christians have likewise distorted the relationship between grace and human actions, as if one precluded the other. These and other splits have often made for a needlessly fractured Christian world.

In spite of these many distortions throughout Christian history, the one decisive split that bears upon every follower of Jesus is that of sin and holiness. They can only be related to each other as opposites. Because sin, in its root, renounces the very meaning of God's revelation in our lives, it can never be reconciled in a Christian life. Christians might quibble endlessly about whether a particular action is a sin, and under what circumstances it is sinful (although most of this quibbling happens when we think of our life as rules and not relationship). But Christians never quibble about the fact that sin is totally out of place in a disciple's life.

So much of modern history rests on a fanaticism of one sort or another—be it communism, Nazism, racism, or some kind of economic imperialism. People from Lenin through Hitler, Idi Amin through Slobadan Milosevic, Rafael Trujillo through Osama Bin Laden, seem perfectly capable of subjecting everything else for the sake of some ideal. Even Christians, through the Inquisition and the Thirty Years' Wars, the "troubles" of Northern Ireland, and the slaughter of Rwanda, have not been exempt from fanaticisms of their own.

Yet we do have to live for something grand, sweeping, compelling. We each have to decide what will be the point of our lives, what we will live in, for...and without.

Fidelity to God's Word asks only one thing of us: To be faithful to the sweep of God's kingdom and to the eradication of sin that is the kingdom's prerequisite.

Questions for Reflection

How do you feel people today develop the standards by which they are to live? In what ways do the images we have about ourselves shape—and distort—those images?

Do you think that modern culture is "narcissistic," that is, modern people live absorbed with themselves and their self image? If so, what are the costs of this personally and socially? What does the "myth of Narcissus" have to teach us?

What do you think are the ideals that God holds up before us, as the mirror in which we are to find ourselves? What qualities of God seem more natural to you? What qualities of God seem more distant and difficult to reflect?

Who would you describe as holy—in your own personal experience? On the contemporary scene? Why? How does your image of holiness reflect a person's relationship with God?

What do you feel people live for most today? In what ways do people grasp the generosity of God? In what ways do people have trouble seeing God's generosity?

What do you feel most people consider sin to be? Comment on that.

Developing Our Discipleship

Every disciple who strives to live in fidelity to God's word must

- daily consider the ideals that God call us to
- daily measure life in terms of God's personal being and qualities
- daily examine life to test its conformity to God's Word
- daily list the ways self-centeredness has taken hold
- daily exercise generosity (of time, resources and self) toward God and others
- daily acknowledge the power of sin and pray for the Spirit's more powerful presence
- daily restrain impulses of sin
- regularly confess sin to God and others
- daily commit oneself to pursuit of holiness.

Find a time and place to examine your life every day. Do this without increasing your self-absorption, but rather increasing your sense of freedom.

Adopt a pattern of personal penance whereby, through action and self-denial, you affirm that you, and your pleasures, are not the center of life, but God and God's people, particularly the poor and suffering.

Exploring the Scriptures

Read Leviticus 19 for an insight into the ways ritual and personal behavior intertwined for the ancient Jewish people.

Read the prophet Hosea and reflect on the images of faithfulness and betrayal which this book gives us.

We mostly think of the letter to the Romans as a difficult lesson about grace, freedom, and salvation. But sections in Romans translate these lofty ideas into reflections of how Christians should live. Read Romans 12—15 for a sense of the kind of relationships early Christians cultivated.

Read Galatians 5 as a way to reflect on the power of the Holy Spirit in freeing us to live God's ideals.

Mapping the Disciple's Path

God's Word and our response in Worship provide standards.

These standards help us to see ourselves without distortion, delusion, or seduction.

These standards hold the promise of making us free.

These standards call us to a life of perfection.

This life makes us want to mirror God's qualities in our actions by which we live in the kingdom, pursuing its values,

for the kingdom, learning trust and generosity,

and without the elements of sin which obscure God.

In this way we are led to:

A life of witness to God and God's kingdom.

Chapter Four

You Shall Witness to the Lord Your God

So what does God ask of us?

"…[Y]ou will be my witnesses in Jerusalem, in all Judea and Samaria, and to the ends of the earth." (Acts 1:8)

"When the Advocate comes, whom I will send to you from the Father, the Spirit of truth who comes from the Father, he will testify on my behalf. You also are to testify because you have been with me from the beginning." (John 15:26–27)

If even lifeless stones and markers have enormous power to communicate the memory of an event or a person, how much more can living people, through their words and actions?

Although people rarely visit cemeteries in modern times, when they do, even the markers of unknown people move those who walk by them. Names, dates, perhaps a descriptive phrase about the life of someone who lived decades ago, fill the imaginations of visitors: all those lives and relationships—how they teach us about the beauty, and fleetingness, of our own lives. They witness to lives past, and present.

Many local communities will also put out crosses or candles where some tragedy has happened. By the bend of a road where a young person died, or at the storefront where a person was murdered, flowers and candles reflect an overflow of sadness and sympathy. One sees wreathes, long weathered, to mark a point of grief. The death scenes of famous people are festooned with items left by thousands who probably never knew the famed in person, but somehow identified with them in life—and now also in death. The flowers, cards, candles, and other markers bear testimony to the life now ended, and the love that still endures.

This happens not only with personages like Princess Diana, whose death stirred great memorials of grief around the world, or a singer like Elvis Presley, some of whose fans refuse to believe he is even dead, but also in poor urban communities when a child's life is cut short through parental abuse, or an innocent youth is shot during a gang fight or perhaps even at the hands of officers of the law. Flowers, cards, candles, posters—all to give witness to the moment.

We see some of this instinct to memorialize moments before us every day. In cities, whenever they lay down new cement, young people strive to engrave some sign of themselves before the cement solidifies; in the more rural areas, lovers carve trees with hearts and initials, making a sign of their love, which often endures longer than the romance itself. Visitors to famous monuments, themselves witnesses to the noble, often find them covered with the graffiti of other visitors, all done in the vain hope of leaving some irrefutable evidence of a distinct moment in time. "John Z. Was Here, 2-22-2000," future visitors read for a dozen years, wondering what motivated John Z. to take marker in hand.

Joshua, having crossed the Jordan in a way that paralleled Moses' crossing of the Red Sea, seeks out large stones on which to make a sacrifice—and which will remain as witnesses to the wonder of God's work among the chosen. "Joshua said to them, 'Pass on before the ark of the LORD your God into the middle of the Jordan, and each of you take up a stone on his shoulder, one for each of the tribes of the Israelites, so that this may be a sign among you. When your children ask in time to come, "What do those stones mean to you?" then you shall tell them that the waters of the Jordan were cut off in front of the ark of the covenant of the LORD. When it crossed over the Jordan, the waters of the Jordan were cut off. So these stones shall be to the Israelites a memorial forever'" (Josh 4:5–7).

Markers, signs, indelible statements, witnesses to something that others wish never to be forgotten. How much of modern sadness has been caught in the Vietnam Memorial in Washington, D.C., or the memorial of chairs in Oklahoma City where a federal building's destruction took one hundred and thirty-four lives, or the way family members clung to every relic of a loved one's memory when the World Trade Center and Pentagon were attacked by terrorists on a cloudless September morning.

How much more, then, is the witness of *living* people—the words and gestures of someone who places him- or herself as a sign of something that should not be forgotten, of something that should command the attention of all.

In My Person

One of the stock drama themes in popular entertainment revolves around people being witnesses in difficult court cases. The drama comes from the risk that a witness sometimes has to take. Such witnesses place their own persons, their own lives, on the line for the sake of affirming what they believe is the truth. Those against whom they testify might resort to intimidation, bribery, or even murder to keep the testimony from happening.

Why? Because there is so much power in the willingness of someone to say what he or she has seen, to put their own selves on the line. Though scientific studies might raise questions about the reliability of eyewitness testimony, all the world knows the power of someone saying, "This is the truth I know, and I am testifying to it."

After all, even if one is convinced of the perceived truth, when placed before others and subject to cross-examination, the bravery of simply asserting a truth exacts its own cost. Did we see what we thought we did? How can we be sure? Might we have other motives in our testimony? Haven't we made mistakes of identity before? Under such a barrage, seeing and knowing no longer look as easy as we often make them out to be.

So the power of someone personally testifying stands against other forces—particularly those of denial and doubt—and often the testimony alone provides some way for society to see things that would otherwise remain invisible or deniable. The truth comes at the cost of our own persons, whether metaphorically or, in tragic instances, literally, as when people are killed to keep them quiet.

In a society when people resist even being jurors, how much less anxious would they be to give testimony, to be witnesses?

And if this is true in cases about money, ambition, or anger, which result in some observable crime, what about being a witness to God whom much of society, whatever surveys report, can so easily dismiss or doubt?

Hypocrisy, the Failure of Witness

If we dwell in God's Word, if we place God at the center of our lives, if we worship God personally and in community, then the truth of God holds claim on us. Believers are called to uphold the truth of God. God calls believers to be witnesses to God's being and absolute love.

In other words, if God is so important in a person's life, where is the evidence for that? One of the great bumper stickers to appear in the late 1980s read: "If you were arrested for being a Christian, would there be any evidence against you?" Although the Scriptures might occasionally speak of the risk of being persecuted for one's beliefs, in today's world that seems almost ludicrous. No one, at least in the Western world, takes faith that seriously, it seems.

One of the temptations of worship, which involves so much exterior sign and ritual, is to substitute the sign for the reality. So great is this danger that no more common thread runs through churches that use ritual then this: Be what you profess, live up to the sign you have received, be worthy of your baptism, your marriage, your being united with the Body of Christ.

What greater embarrassment can there be for faith than when whole sectors of believers, having been baptized or confirmed, live as if nothing of the Gospel ever happened in their lives? The ceremony happens, the rites are celebrated, relatives bring the gifts and cards, the medals are worn, but life continues as unreformed as ever. Whether it's Puccini drawing hypocrisy in bold form through the cynical figure of Scarpia in the opera *Tosca*, or Francis Ford Coppola pushing hypocrisy in our faces on the wide screen in *The Godfather* saga, we know what it is to say one thing with our mouths and something else with our deeds. "Do you renounce Satan?" As the Godfather answers "Yes," the bullets start to fly.

The charge of hypocrisy, leveled by many against those who are "church going," grows in proportion to the ideal. The "punk" seems more grotesque when he once was "a choir boy," and the embezzling secretary greedier when she was the "church's devoted worker." They join in scandal those clergy who, with their church robes barely removed, abuse the trust of their congregants—even their children—through misdeeds. All these holy people who didn't live up to what they professed!

From Dante and Chaucer down to modern times, hypocritical believers have been spoofed—and not merely for their failures, the pecadillos or foibles. All humans have those. Rather their failures stand out all the more because they contrast with the noble ideals for which they should have stood. More than just failure, hypocrisy is betrayal of what should have been upheld, even at great personal cost

But hypocrisy, whether it's deliberate or from just human inadvertence, does at least tell us what the case should be. The failure does reveal the ideal. We know from the convicted minister how a minister should act.

If hypocrisy is saying one thing and doing something else, then witness is the reverse. Being a witness lines our lives up with our words, our deeds, and our avowals of faith.

Standing Up

Most people, when asked how they live out their faith, will answer with a string of negatives. "I don't cheat on my wife, I don't cheat on my taxes. I don't skip my prayers too often. I don't have any enemies." In other words, standing up for one's faith often means the least common denominator, with "least" being emphasized. People who have made commitments somehow feel that the minimal attempt to live up to that commitment is more than enough. Married people will feel themselves quite justified if they have not committed adultery, no matter how much indifference or coldness otherwise characterizes their marriage. Others will feel "not getting drunk or using drugs" gives them a hallowed position in life. One thinks one has stood up and been a witness so long as one has not abandoned the faith—or corrupted it too much.

It's true that only few people abandon their faith outright, perhaps because for most their faith is not very important to begin with—it isn't even worth abandoning! They never think about it that much. Most believers, instead of abandonment, craftily compromise the living of their faith. They carefully read the opinions of others—what will not be too much of a scandal—and weave their faith around that. Being nice, being accommodating, not upsetting the apple cart, doing only what others expect, makes many believers feel they are doing what is right.

Instead of living faith, these believers are living "faith-lite"—the lowest common denominator. Only this kind of "faith-lite" can explain the massive failure of faith seen in the lifetimes of many contemporaries, when millions of Christians stood by as whole segments of their fellow humans, their fellow countrymen, were killed. How gingerly self-styled Christians must read their witness to faith when it allows them to tolerate, or at least to block out, the least defensible of atrocities. What happened to the Jewish people in Germany, France, Spain, Poland, and even Italy, was replicated by what happened to many ethnic groups in the Balkans, and also what happened to so many in the Tutsi tribe in Rwanda. True, in these instances powerful social forces influenced people who perhaps were confused or stunned into inaction; nevertheless, these social forces had more power than the Gospel.

Perhaps the witness to our faith will not always call for bravery, but it certainly always calls for backbone, for being a living testimony, for asserting the truth, even when that might cost. Our modern, pluralistic societies insidiously make "being accommodating" the most important quality. Surely being a witness to faith hardly means annoying and insulting others in the name of one's beliefs; nevertheless, it clearly also means more than "we all should be nice to each other."

In the face of compromise, the figures of Dietrich Bonhoeffer, Maximilian Kolbe, Edith Stein, Otto Schindler, Martin Luther King, Jr., Archbishop Oscar Romero, Mother Teresa of Calcutta, and Yitzhak Rabin—to mention only a few modern witnesses—raise an entirely other alternative. Each of these people faced a critical choice, a moment when the stakes of their life decision became very clear, when the prospect of extreme suffering and even death loomed as a likely course. Each of them could well have justified turning back from the course upon which they set out. Yet each of them maintained an integrity to the central truth that life unfolded for them—and they did this in the face of opposition. They acted not by disrespecting others, but by seeking a greater justice, a deeper peace, a fuller kindness, which could appeal to all.

Although the stakes of few lives are as high as in the lives of these men and women, we all face times when we are tempted to flinch away from witness. What of the way so many believers swallow what is important to them rather than speak up in a difficult situation? What of the ways we hide our faith, or even our religious allegiance, because that makes us feel more comfortable before others. Some believers will even hide their religious allegiance in cultures where speaking from one's faith tradition, such as the American South, is quite permissible. How rare for today's believers to pray thanksgiving over their meals when in restaurants. "I hope you don't embarrass us by saying grace."

Modern democracies perhaps frown on faith being too prominent in public life; it always seem to be a major point of contention. However, the more telling question might be whether faith is prominent even in our private lives, in our homes, among our friends, within the circle of our closest associates. We might more freely show our faith tactfully in public settings if we lived our faith deeply in the private settings of our lives.

Witnesses are not afraid to stand up because the truth to which they testify does not lie outside them, in the opinions others have; it lies within them, in what they have come to affirm and value. And when witness is done with the correct motivation—to reveal the truth and not to belittle others—it affirms and values the good in all human existence. The truth of the Gospel does not dismiss the experience of other people. Being a witness does not mean being a fanatic. The fanatic witnesses to values, surely, but in a destructive way that closes off access to others. The witness for the kingdom upholds the values of the kingdom particularly as these are revealed already in the lives of people. It creates access for people into the vision of the kingdom.

Ministry

One large growth in Christian life in the last fifty years has been the movement of believers toward ministry. The apostolate, personal ministry, the power of lay people in the world, has received much reflection and attention in recent decades.

It is a common thing today, for example, to find lay people in a parish involved in many aspects of the parish's life—even in roles that once seemed the enclave of the clergy. The status of "lay ecclesial ministers" has become a formal way to designate those people who have an official, credential place of leadership in the church—directors of religious education, for example, or pastoral associates. Beyond these, thousands of Christians have made ministry part of the way they witness to their faith—through public reading of the scriptures at worship, to teaching about faith to children and adults, to visiting the poor or consoling the bereaved.

This growth has placed a proportionate challenge before lay ministers as well—to have their ministry reflected in the rest of their lives. For witness is hardly reserved to what we say or do in church. Unfortunately, far too many believers act like "church mice"—comfortable only around their own, secure only in their small circle of faith. The intensity of our worship or feeling does not demonstrate our faith; that is demonstrated by the way the vision of the kingdom grows in the world.

God demands that we be witnesses to those subtle and mighty deeds that constitute the kingdom of grace that Jesus advanced and brought to fulfillment. These deeds have broken into our individual lives for we have all experienced forgiveness and healing. They also need to touch all existence because God's deeds would draw everything toward absolute love.

Jesus was the center of the life of one particular woman who died about a dozen years ago. More than a volunteer in her parish, she embodied care for every segment of society that she faced. After a long day's work, it was a joy to teach religion to the neighborhood's poorer children. Seniors felt abandoned and disconnected because of their limited lives; this woman would connect them to the parish and to local social services. From organizing a large dinner on Thanksgiving for the aged and lonely, to bringing Holy Communion to the sick on her block, this woman was eager to serve. Selflessly, generously, with humor and graciousness, she touched thousands of people by the simplicity and directness of her faith. Her attention to others gave her many opportunities to invite people back to church, or suggest to people that they consider following Christ as believers. She asked nothing for herself; she gave even before others could make a request. She radiated Christ and lived in his Spirit. People saw Christ on her face. She was a witness.

We witness to God's saving deeds when we let them shape our lives; and when we make our lives markers, undeniable signs, of God's grace present in the world. How does Jesus put it when he is on his way to death? "I tell you, if these were silent, the stones would shout out" (Luke 19:40).

Too bad the stones had to cry out. Why were the people so silent? And why are Christians today?

Questions for Reflection

Reflect on the human need to memorialize important experiences. Where does this come from? What are the values that these memorials bring to life? How different would life be without these monuments?

Have you ever given witness in a formal way? Do you know anyone who has? What has the experience been like? What have you felt when you served as a juror?

Who do people claim that church is filled with so many hypocrites? Is hypocrisy almost unavoidable? Examine the difference between people who only appear to hold ideals and those who try to uphold them, but fail.

What has been the cost of scandal and noted public failures among believers? How can this be redressed by believers?

What is the hardest part of being a witness to faith? When is being a witness easier? How have you experienced the witness of others? What has been attractive, and what has been problematic?

What is the connection between witness and ministry in the church? What new challenges does being a minister place on believers?

Developing Our Discipleship

Discover ways in which you hide your faith. Analyze the reasons. Commit yourself to reversing this in certain specific ways.

Review your situation at work, in the neighborhood, with the family. Uncover opportunities to stand up for your faith and values in a manner that does not condemn or deprecate the faith of others.

Tactfully raise issues with others that call for a review of attitudes concerning evils that society simply denies. Think of economic or social injustices. Find out how to raise these issues effectively and persuasively.

Inventory your life to find the things that contradict the values you uphold—whether it be music, television, film, or books—and make decisions about them. What do you tolerate that really stands in contradiction to the basics of your faith? What can you modify, what can you change?

Examine your life each day, asking in what ways you have stood up for the kingdom of God.

Read and study the lives of people who have been witnesses to their faith. Enter into a spiritual dialogue with them, seeking to appropriate their values.

Review periodically the "works of mercy" that have guided Christian life and witness for centuries. How are these part of the witness of your life as a disciple?

Spiritual Works of Mercy	*Corporal Works of Mercy*
Feed the hungry	Share your knowledge
Give drink to the thirsty	Give counsel to the needy
Clothe the naked	Comfort the sorrowing
Care for the sick	Show patience with others
Visit the imprisoned	Forgive those who offend
Bury the dead	Admonish those in error

Exploring the Scriptures

Read Deuteronomy, chapters 1–6 for a vision of the kind of following of God that developed among the ancient Hebrews.

Explore the imagery of the parables in Matthew 13 for its bearing on witnessing faithfully in our lives.

Read Matthew 25 for his view of the final judgment; what does this say about where the emphasis of our witness should be?

Mapping the Disciple's Path

If God's Word and our response in worship lead us
to a life of fidelity to God,
then God's truth will have an essential claim on our lives.

Disciples reveal the impact of God's truth by the
witness of their lives—
how they put themselves on the line, and how they avoid the
betrayal of hypocrisy.

Disciples live out what their worship says
about them by their actions—
in the way they speak out, bring faith into their
social and personal worlds,
and create access for others to faith.

This leads disciples, beyond witness,

To proclaim their faith to the world.

Chapter Five

You Shall Proclaim the Word of God

What does God expect of the disciples of Jesus?

> And Jesus came and said to [the eleven], "All authority in heaven and on earth has been given to me. Go therefore and make disciples of all nations, baptizing them in the name of the Father and of the Son and of the Holy Spirit, and teaching them to obey everything that I have commanded you…" (Matt 28:18–20).

> "Therefore whatever you have said in the dark will be heard in the light, and what you have whispered behind closed doors will be proclaimed from the housetops" (Luke 12:3).

Where does the impulse to share good news come from? Imagine someone who won a large prize, say in a state lottery or even a church raffle. Imagine the kind of reaction when the news first comes—"I think I have those winning numbers," or "I actually won the minivan the church was raffling off!" Enter into the initial disbelief—how the winner reviews the numbers again and again, matching them against the figures printed in the newspaper, how the winner questions the messenger again and again. "You're not kidding me, aren't you? I can't believe it."

What happens next? If the prize is indeed substantial, the winner might start consulting lawyers or accountants, attempting to get a handle on some of the implications of this windfall. But who else gets told? And how? With these questions we come against a fundamental dynamic inside every "good news" story: It simply wants to be told.

For even if the winner of a huge amount should decide to keep it secret because "I don't want everyone in the phone book calling me up," we know, without question, that this lucky person must tell someone. The message simply cannot be contained. Enter into this mental state: Someone knows something that changes everything about his or her life. This stays a secret? At the very least, because of the change involved, the winner has to say something to those most bound up with his or her life—closest relatives and friends. "You're not going to believe this, but..."

Or even if someone has won a large but not life-changing prize, notice the dynamic still. Everyone in the church will want to know who won the minivan. They'll want to know if it was "someone we knew, a parishioner, that won." And, if not, who? Should they not have had the luck to win, who did? They want to share in the good news. But the winner also wants to share the good news. "Guess what?" he says. "I won," she says. Why?

In some way it's because the smiling of outrageous fortune on any one person says something about the smiling of fortune on everyone and everything. However bad we imagine life to be, however unjust, however filled with stress or conflict, some things happen that show how else life can be or, in fact, how else life actually is, at least every now and then.

Good news is for everyone. Because good news not only changes the life of the one who wins, it changes the fabric of human existence itself.

Perhaps we might imagine it this way: Every now and then a veil is removed and we see the glory, the joy, that stalks us, though we mostly do not allude to it.

If, indeed, revelations of sheer horror, and stories about the abject cruelty that humans can show to others, demonstrate the darkness that lurks in human life, these moments of good news make, perhaps, an even greater claim on the human spirit. They portray a deeper truth: We may experience utter terror during our lives, but we were made, ultimately, to experience joy. Stories of good news bring us home to this truth about ourselves.

Good News

We hear good news against the backdrop of our lives—one that makes the hearing of good news sound different depending on our experiences. If the truth of our lives is that, despite some of life's evidence, we were destined to experience joy, and good news brings us to this realization, then the rest of our experiences colors the sense of joy we might anticipate.

Many people in modern life, for example, appear to feel quite content about themselves and their lives. Apart from the arrival of serious illness or the unexpected loss of a loved one, people feel their personal and professional lives are going well. Modern civilization has progressed enough that many people in the developed world can expect a decent wage, a roof over their heads, some kind of relational security with a loved one, and plenty of diversion from today's burgeoning entertainment industry. "Don't Worry, Be Happy," was a popular song in the early 90s; it makes a good theme song for our whole generation as well.

If life is so good, then why do we need good news? Or, more particularly, why do we need the Good News of the Gospel of Jesus Christ?

On the other hand, modern people, for all the contentment they feel, appear also to have a tremendous sense of brokenness, seemingly more than past generations which did not enjoy the benefits of health and technology we do today. Large percentages of contemporary folk could sing, without missing a beat, the popular hymn, "Amazing Grace."

Amazing Grace, how sweet the sound
That saved a wretch like me;
I once was lost, but now am found,
Was blind but now I see.

These somewhat astonishing words stand in stark contrast to the optimism and "feel good" spunk that much of modern life puts out—I'm OK, life is full of opportunities, I have the skills to do anything I want. Unaccountably, amid all the hoopla, "Amazing Grace" is probably one of the most frequently sung hymns. Behind today's "feelgoodism," there apparently lies a great sense of feeling lost and blind, of feeling like a wretch. Perhaps most of what gets sung or presented in sitcoms is sheer fraud and everyone feels out of sync with it. Or perhaps certain souls need, to use the image of the early American psychologist, William James, to be "twice born" because their first life is broken and needs the total repair of divine grace.

In this case, "Good News" can be put very clearly: the Gospel of Jesus—the story of his brokenness and his resurrection—is applied personally and psychologically to our own, particular living drama. We experience, by identifying with the Gospel, a powerful release from what blinds and binds us, be that addiction, shameful life habits, an overwhelming sense of failure, repeated and serious sin, or the psychological insecurities that sometimes beset even the most gifted of us. Many people who identify themselves as "evangelicals" point to just such an experience of "being saved" as proof of God's grace. In fact, they often see the absence of such an experience as proof of the absence of God's grace in a life.

These evangelical people—and they span a rather large chunk of Christians who do not belong to "mainline" churches—seemingly have the easiest time proclaiming their faith to others because their faith has become so intertwined with their personal life drama of brokenness and repair, a drama which they believe everyone undergoes, whether they know it or not.

Yet if the broken can hear Good News so clearly in personal terms, what of those who don't feel themselves so broken? Is God's Good News inaudible to them? Have they nothing to hear? Or proclaim?

In fact, a whole other stream of Christian thought has developed another way of thinking about Good News—not primarily from human brokenness, but rather from the experience of human longing and desire. It isn't that people are depraved and corrupt; it is that, however much they have, they still are incomplete. And, without God, they will remain incomplete. In other words, even apart from sin, depravity, brokenness, and shame, people still need the Good News of God because their very hearts, filled with beauty and joy, experience these only as anticipation of something more, something fuller and greater, which they desperately need to make sense of their lives.

Whatever the beauty and comfort of our lives, they dissolve in frustration. Our loves, passionate though they be, still run the risk of coldness and separation. Our songs, light and happy though they be, all come at some point to their final verse. Our eyes, filled with the beauty of a dawn or of a beloved's face, still will grow dim. Our lives, sated with friendship and happiness, still will end in death. In the words of the song the late Peggy Lee made famous, "Is that all there is?"

This way of stating the Gospel—that God restores us to wholeness and brings us to the fullness for which we long—speaks very powerfully to the whole situation of our human existence, whoever we are and however much we have. The Gospel, in this way, is not heard primarily as a response to personal crisis (though it really is that), but as a horizon that looms as hope for all human flesh. It is a universal, cosmic drama, as well as a personal one. Someone like St. Thomas Aquinas in the thirteenth century saw this as a whole pattern to understand human existence—our coming forth from God and our return to God. His contemporary, St. Bonaventure, likewise saw a pattern—human existence as a journey toward God.

The death and resurrection of Jesus speak to the utter frustration of our elusive human existence, to the absurdity of so much grandeur going nowhere, to the quest of our spirit for eternal Spirit, to participate in the very being of God. The ancient writers of the Greek Christian tradition, like St. Gregory or St. Basil, referred to this as "divinization"—the marvel of our sharing God's own life through the Spirit of Jesus. In this reading, Jesus dies to expose the frailty and frustration of our lives; he rises to transcend that frailness; and he sends the Spirit so that we can partake of the very reality of his risen life, being body in his Body and living in his very life. "It is no longer I who live," says St. Paul, "but it is Christ who lives in me" (Gal 2:20).

The disciple of Jesus has the duty to proclaim God's Good News in both its forms, as it speaks to our personal brokenness and also as it speaks to our human incompleteness. Both these forms of gospel proclamation challenge the illusion that "this life is enough," and both of them face the stiff competition of alternative myths which today make no room for the Gospel. The gravest danger to Christian faith comes from that myth which says that we have no need for Good News at all.

All people are in need of salvation. This means we all need a help and remedy from beyond ourselves, which can only come from God, to free us from the consequences of our not living in God—sin, meaninglessness in life, and death without any hope. Whether people feel themselves broken, or whether they feel fine about themselves, they all stand under what St. Paul calls the "wrath" of God. This word, so difficult to grasp in detail, refers to the ultimate judgment that results from our estrangement from God. That estrangement, with us from our birth, means that we live egoistically for ourselves and not with lives centered on God (see, for example, Rom 1:18, 2:8).

To proclaim Good News is to bring the one message that changes everything in human life—a message of wholeness, forgiveness, grace, peace, unity, love, and transcendence beyond death. To proclaim Good News is to announce something far more important than human luck or unexpectedly great wealth. It verifies the hope built into every human heart, the goodness that underlies every dream, the instinctual resistance to oppression, that human cry for life that, in the face of death, simply will not be exterminated.

Bringing the Message

But how, in practice, do we proclaim God's Good News? What are the preliminaries and the dynamics?

Designed as we are to exchange words in a context of trust, disciples of Jesus cannot bring Good News without first establishing a relationship of trust with someone else. This relationship must be free, genuine, open, and nonmanipulative. It must flow from the power of simple human encounter, when people behold each other with respect and esteem. If it is based on anything else, it simply is not a true relationship.

Because of this needed relationship, the message cannot be proclaimed in such a way that we dismiss or dismantle the experience of others. How often believers think they are evangelizing by disturbing and dismissing the faith that someone already has! Some evangelizers in this vein think nothing of approaching people coming out of one church, attacking their faith on false terms ("You worship idols"), and creating human expectations that, in effect, entrap a person. Evangelization cannot mean setting out to recycle people, as often happens today, from one Christian community to another. Such methods only feed on the uncertainties that people may feel about themselves rather than on the strengths with which the Spirit would work.

The one who proclaims Good News must attend to the opportune moment when, whether from need or curiosity or desire, someone's heart opens to hear a new message. How much friendship, goodwill, and respect must be present before this moment can come! And how much the witness of a believer's life makes the sharing of faith, tactfully, and respectfully, possible. So the disciple, whose life witnesses the Good News, has to learn to read the signs and grasp the moments in which to speak, knowing that God's Spirit is already at work.

The preparatory steps before proclaiming Good News include human encounter, friendship, witness, dialogue, and invitation. Cultivating these with a genuine heart that seeks the good of the other person, disciples can share with another their personal stories of faith, and the central story of the death and resurrection of Jesus Christ. They can also witness to the essential place played by the Church and its worship. Sometimes it may take but a few moments for another's heart to open; sometimes it may take years. In all instances, it takes a profound respect for where the other person is, and a trust in God's grace.

Evelyn Waugh, in his famous novel *Brideshead Revisited,* uses a powerful image: God is the master fisherman who places the smallest hook in the mouths of each of us. He lets us swim here and there, but all the while tugging gently at our hearts; finally, when our flight has exhausted us, God ever so gently pulls the tip of the pole, sets the hook, and begins to reel us in.

Perhaps this is why Jesus chose fishermen to follow him—he knew the patience proclaimers of the Good News would need.

The Proclamation

The Christian Scriptures are instructive of how Good News comes. Much attention is usually given to the book of Acts, where

Peter, Stephen, and Paul give powerful and polished proclamations to hearers who are swept off their feet in faith—or who reject the word to their own detriment. Such scenes from Acts depict in a stylistic way, with great drama, the various kinds of proclamations and strategies that early believers undertook.

However, apart from the book of Acts, the Gospels also give a rich vein of data about other, less stylized, ways in which the Good News happens—through the compassionate presence of Jesus Christ in the lives of those in need. In the Gospels, which are systematically read in most mainline Christian churches on Sunday, we see Jesus approaching people in various states of need, whether physical (through healing and even resurrection), psychological (through the call to change), intellectual (through teaching), and esthetic (by the beauty of wisdom sayings or the parables).

Here we can see the varied approach, focused on the needs of individuals, which Jesus and the early church employed—and which disciples today can apply in their own everyday experience. The truth about proclamation and conversion is that the Gospel spreads along peer networks, through human relationships already established, in which people come to know the needs of others and can respond to them appropriately and without manipulation. This helps us understand why Paul kept up his trade as a tent-maker and repairer of leather goods—it allowed him to maintain a peer network from which he worked to spread Good News (see 1 Cor 4:11–12).

What and how the disciple proclaims depend not only on the need of the other, but also on the rich and varied elements of a full Christian life. As people reveal their own worries, fears, and frustrations, so different aspects of the Gospel can be opened to them. From that, the depths of the Scriptures unfold: the great themes from the Hebrew Scriptures; the power of the prophets' hope; the passion and peace of the psalms; the challenge of the Wisdom books like Job, Ecclesiastes, or Proverbs. There is so much with which to feed another, the disciple trusts the Spirit to reveal the layers of hunger in a searcher's life. For some, conversion will come as healing, for others as homecoming, for others as discovery, for others as a grasp for true beauty.

At the same time, proclamation is hardly a private conversation between two people. The disciple proclaims as a member of a believing community. Being in community, in worship, prayer, and mutual support, is part of the Gospel which is being imparted. The disciple who proclaims Good News also invites another into community, into relationship with the Church which the Scriptures, with good reason, call the "Body of Christ" (Rom 12:4ff.; 1 Cor 10:7; 1 Cor 12:12ff.; Eph 1:22–23; 3:6; Col 1:18). The Christian Scriptures do not let us ignore the relationship between the body of Jesus Christ, the body which is given as food in the Eucharist, and the body of the community of believers (see 1 Cor 11:24–29). To encounter Christ, one must engage with his living body, in the Church and its worship. Only in relation to the body is the Holy Spirit given.

So proclamation of the Gospel ultimately means that a disciple, fed at the table of Jesus Christ, invites and helps another discover a place at the same table. It means that a disciple, living the life of the Spirit through prayer and personal transformation, involves another in the disciplines of the same Spirit (see Gal 5:16–23.) Proclamation means helping someone encounter the whole mystery that Jesus reveals, the three-person God who loves and saves, the dying and rising that the Spirit brings about, and the way of life that embodies these truths.

Our popular images of St. Paul seduce us to think of evangelization in perhaps primarily marketing or sales categories. His restlessness and intensity, his boldness and willingness to confront, seem both admirable—and offputting! Yet behind all those images lies the story of one who met up with a community of faith, was sent back to that community of faith after a powerful breakdown, and built up communities of faith gradually through his relationships with others as a friend and coworker. Paul, as noted previously, was a skilled laborer, a worker in leather goods, hanging out with others in the same guild. Paul's visit to synagogues were hardly like visiting a modern congregation. Rather, synagogues were adult meeting centers where people shared their insights and experiences in light of the Scriptures. Paul, in other words, used the human dynamics open to all disciples—his skills, his peer network, his ongoing discoveries, and his love of Jesus Christ.

Proclaiming

If there's anything that many Christians shy away from, it is the obligation of proclaiming faith. "You don't want us to visit homes, to knock on doors?" is the first reaction of many when they hear of evangelization. So dominant has the modern quality of minding one's own business become, that believers feel that any attempt to share faith somehow intrudes on another's freedom. "You're not shoving your faith down my throat," has become the great whip that drives many a believer back into a corner.

This aversion comes, mostly, from the poor and improper evangelization that has become the main model most people have when they think of sharing faith. It comes from the way believers have themselves been treated when, in the name of Jesus, they themselves are accosted by others who belittle their faith or dismiss their own religious experience. It comes from marketing techniques that may seem clever and may even be effective in attracting bodies, but that do not respect the human, interpersonal dimension that always accompanies authentic evangelization.

It comes from models of evangelization that have no place for ecumenism, that do not realize that the efforts of Christians to understand each other are themselves processes of conversion. It comes from assumptions of evangelists that people are wretched and full of shame because they believe that conversion only happens when it results as a call from brokenness and depravity. It comes from the smugness that the saved often feel—a smugness built up at the expense of others.

But proclamation, as Jesus sent the disciples forward, does not entail any of these negative traits. It only entails the human dynamic of sharing Good News with others as they are capable of hearing it and responding to it. In spreading faith, tact is just as important as zeal, as one wise evangelist once put it.

Many believers, particularly from mainline Christian communions, feel inadequate about sharing faith because they have not learned some memorized script that reputedly leads another to Christ. Actually, though, every believer can retrieve from his or her personal experience the outlines of a story of faith as compelling and as sincere as Christian sharing has been from its beginnings. And every believer can put together in a simple way the key truths of his or her faith in Christ so that another person can grasp them.

But the central resource for evangelizing is not how much of the Catechism one has memorized or how much Scripture one has digested. Rather, the simple power of a life of faith, lived and shared, becomes the bag of seeds that God uses to sow in today's world. No one can predict what will come from those seeds, only that the proclaimer will continue to sow them, without presumption and without discouragement, simply because there is so much overabundance to share (see Matt 13:1ff., and Mark 4:1ff.).

If in our "post-Christian" world, religion seems almost quaint, in the "pre-Christian" world of Justin, in the second century, religion was lived with risk. Himself a multicultural man, of Greek ancestors growing up in Samaria, Justin was a searcher for the truth. Having sought the teachings of the philosophers and religions of his day, he met an aging believer who ended Justin's search by the compelling message of God's work in Jesus Christ. Justin traveled, instructed many people in the faith, wrote defenses on behalf of Christians—and did all this while seeing the best in everything around him. He saw the work of Jesus everywhere present in those seeds of goodness and salvation that Jesus scattered throughout human experience from the beginning of creation. He rooted his life in the Scriptures (he quotes many of the Bible's books even at this early state), in baptism and the Eucharist, and insisted that a believer's life did not take away from society, but only enriched it. Arrested as many Christians were during the time of Marcus Aurelius, he proclaimed his faith in the face of certain death. Having found the truth of his life, he could hardly deny it.

Justin lived in a world filled with many choices and possible directions. In this he was like us. Unlike most of us, he was willing to risk everything for the sake of the Good News he found. With so much Good News, and with its life-changing message, how could he keep it to himself?

For that matter, how can we?

Questions for Reflection

Explore some memories of "good news" events in your life. What was it like to hear good news, to tell it to another? What created the excitement or the urgency?

What are the ways you have come to understand the grace of God in your own life? In what ways do you understand your life as broken, but now restored? As corrupted, but now made whole? In what ways do you understand your experience as a search for fullness that can only come from God?

How is the Gospel of Jesus Christ Good News for you? To what parts of your own personality has it spoken? What would you say is the main appeal of the Gospel for you?

If you were to share your faith with another, what would you emphasize in terms of your own personal experience?

How have you been able to address the needs of others through your own faith life? Who are your peers (neighbors and friends) who have shown signs of searching? How have you shared with them?

Developing Our Discipleship

Identify your own story of faith, how it came to you, how it is sustained, and how it has shaped your life. Try to write it out.

Grasp the teaching of the Church in simple and understandable ways; try to develop a summary of faith that speaks both to human needs and the broad scope of belief (i.e., the creed). See if you can write the basics of faith on one page.

Be involved in faith-sharing groups to develop your ability to articulate your experience as a believer.

Continue to notice people who have talked to you about your religious practice or your faith. Follow-up on their questions and curiosity.

Reflect on people you know who might be seeking for faith. Spend lots of time trying to enter their experience.

Be involved in the evangelizing activities of your parish—how these activities invite others, how they spread news about the catechumenate that introduces people to Christian life, how they welcome and accept newcomers.

Be attentive to opportunities among your peers, in the workplace or at play, who might be searching for the Gospel.

Review your own need for salvation as a way to sensitize you to the need of others.

Exploring the Scriptures

Read some of the stories about Elijah and Elisha from 1 Kings 17—2 Kings 13. In what ways do the Gospel narrations about Jesus echo the hope and optimism that these prophets brought to ancient Israel?

Read the role of Jeremiah as a prophet of God, particularly as it affected his vision of himself (Jer 1:4–11; 20:7ff.; 26).

Study Paul's understanding of his call in Galatians 2. Read the account of Paul's conversion in Acts (chapter 9 or 22).

Review one of the accounts of the passion and resurrection of Jesus in the Gospels.

Mapping the Disciple's Path

God's Word and worship's response, once it becomes
the standard of our life,
makes a claim on us, but also on all human existence.

God's Good News speaks to human brokenness,
but also to human longing.

The witness of a disciple's life leads to proclamation,
the appropriate sharing of faith.

This sharing happens in human encounter,
in trust and love, at moments when
human needs are disclosed.

It happens when disciples bring their personal stories of faith,
and the church's witness of faith to others,
in sincerity, without manipulation.

Proclaiming Good News leads the disciple to:

Carry the burdens of others.

Chapter Six

You Shall Carry the Burdens of Others

What does God ask of us?

> Let love be genuine; hate what is evil, hold fast to what is good; love one another with mutual affection; outdo one another in showing honor. Do not lag in zeal, be ardent in spirit, serve the Lord. Rejoice in hope, be patient in suffering, persevere in prayer. Contribute to the needs of the saints; extend hospitality to strangers. Bless those who persecute you; bless and do not curse them. Rejoice with those who rejoice, weep with those who weep. (Rom 12:9–15)

> Beloved, let us love one another, because love is from God; everyone who loves is born of God and knows God. Whoever does not love does not know God, for God is love. (1 John 4:7–8)

Numerous studies and commentaries on modern life show a pronounced trend toward individualism. People in technologically advanced societies, for all the new means of communicating with others, seem further apart. We exchange data, leave messages, chat over cell phones, and wear beepers, but the kind of presence we have toward each other seems, for all that, so much weaker.

Societies that rely less on technology have a kind of kinship forced upon them. People have to hang together for safety, for cooperative efforts like farming and marketing, or to raise children in extended families. Before many of our homes became castles—and highly fortified ones at that—they were, in earlier times, enclaves of welcome and hospitality. Children and elderly were cared for by some common sense of community; what happened to any child was of concern to almost any adult.

Whereas individualism has certainly maximized certain aspects of freedom, it has diminished a sense of belonging. The individual today enjoys the possibility of shaping his or her world in accord with one's preferences. There's no need to go shopping because items can be ordered by phone or computer; ever-larger trucking companies bring them right to our door. Nor is there a need, with fast-food vendors and frozen dinners, to even share meals with each other. The TV dinner, zapped in the microwave, sits steaming on the TV tray; people eat, at times in each other's presence, with eyes glued to the tube.

Not so long ago most sports were played by groups—baseball, football, and volleyball, for example. We'd sign up for leagues to play softball or to bowl. Now many who wish exercise run solo for miles, CDs or tapes playing in the runner's ear. Why suffer the inconvenience of having to play a sport at a particular time in a league when we can join gyms and clubs to provide an exercise machine whenever we want? Stationary, we run, the belt rolling under our feet; meters tell us how much we've "biked" or "skied," though we've gone no where. Exercise machines help us tighten our muscles and strengthen our heart—and all of this is done alone, no one intruding on our time or space.

At sporting events we belong to crowds and never know who is rooting and shouting next to us. We shop in malls with the wall of our anonymity breached only when a merchant calls for our credit card information. Our children know each other at school, but parents hardly. Many of our homes have a television for each family member, absolving them of any need to even sit together in the same room. When we worship, we often do so anonymously, afraid that our pastor or fellow parishioner might ask something of us. We rush from our congregations to our private cars and private lives with the taste of the communion wafer ironically lingering in our mouths.

Disciples

All of this individualism directly assaults discipleship. Because disciples do not come as singles, sealed in plastic. Disciples come in groups, in units that make up community. Whether it's the family, the small faith-sharing group, a ministry or church association, disciples who follow Jesus Christ, by definition, do so together. For it is the one Jesus Christ to whom disciples are bound, and the one Spirit of Jesus who binds his followers together.

Long centuries of reflection, which St. Paul began, on the body of Christ have sharpened and expanded meanings contained in this image. Jesus' own body, after his birth and death, is raised in glory. This risen body becomes the instrument of salvation for all who are joined with him. Joining with him makes us part of his body, his church, which extends his presence through time. The

Spirit of Jesus acts to form and energize the body, making it Christ's instrument. In the body we see ourselves as part of Christ and part of each other. Through the body, our strengths and weaknesses are shared, because the members of the body bear each other's burdens as much as they share each other's successes. Jesus lives in himself and in his living body, the Church, forging a union that makes a mockery of individualism.

Individualism, to be sure, differs from the respect that is due to every individual. Disciples prize the individual but reject individualism as a deadly poison. Caring for the individual is, in itself, an affirmation of the bonds that tie us together. Individualism, on the other hand, either resists any ties or shapes them to the preferences of the self, the ego. Care for the individual affirms that every person is a sacred center; individualism affirms oneself as the center—and others primarily as they interest us. The result is a world that views every person as a holder of rights on the basis of which claims can be made and borders enforced. Behold our new world—individuals protecting themselves from each other, demarcating limits from each other, and suing each when limits are breached.

Every great religious tradition and every great philosophy has pointed out the connection that people have with each other; many have gone beyond that to point out the connection that people have with the earth as well. This connectedness has a lot to do with the capacity people have for God—to be unable to see the connection with others certainly prevents an ability to have unity with God. Whereas all great religious traditions cry out for compassion, mercy, and peace, in the Christian writings, loving another as oneself is linked with loving God (Matt 22:37; Mark 12:30; Luke 12:27). The first Letter of John asks how we can claim to love God whom we cannot see when we do not love our brothers and sisters who are plainly visible (1 John 4:20).

Some world traditions base this connection on an inherent unity between people: The humanity of another is an aspect of my own humanity, and vice versa. It's a kind of mystical blending of all experience. Other traditions, however, do not talk of an inherent unity, but rather a "virtual," "as if," unity: *From my own experience* I can tell how another is affected and should be treated. Whether some greater existence holds us together, or whether our individual capacity to relate to others creates a bond, the great poet's insistence that "no man is an island, entire in himself" underlies human civilization. This is the primal truth which Jesus' vision of the kingdom of God reinforces.

St. Paul's image of the body of Christ, while upholding the distinctness of every person, still ties people together in the body of Jesus Christ where the pain of one is the pain of all, and the joy of one is the joy of all (1 Cor 12:26).

Our Burdens

Much of today's sin certainly arises from rejection of the relationship people have with each other. Individualism's greatest temptation is to treat others apart from one's self because our own "self" is the only thing that counts. As a consequence, one treats others as things, objects to be used, events that make no claim on one's soul. A further consequence emerges because others, as things, can be used and hurt. To the extent that we feel little bond with others, we lack the capacity to acknowledge what is happening in the other, and the capacity to cease hurting the other.

We see children grow as they learn their connectedness to others. They fight with their sisters and brothers in a tug-of-war of self-centeredness and stinginess. This shocks us because we imagine children as innocent. They tease animals and wreak destruction on insects because these look like "things" to them—like their own toys or pieces of their games. With good upbringing, however, children are disciplined beyond their self-centeredness until they learn compassion, to grasp the pain of another as their own pain, the experiences of others as reverential moments of growth.

Sharing good experiences comes easily and naturally for most; it's the painful ones that have a harder time making a claim on our souls. Certainly most human beings are instinctually repelled by the outright pain of others; we all cringe when we see, for example, a child being beaten or an old woman mugged. But just as certainly, we anesthetize ourselves from the pain of those around us—growing distant from their inner struggles and cold in the presence of their needs—even with those closest to us. God insists that Christ's disciples bear the burdens of others. The heart of Christian faith is that God bore our burdens in the life and death of Jesus Christ, making our experience, particularly the darker side of our suffering, divine experience.

What is there in the very sharing of burdens that advances humanity toward fullness and the kingdom? The first and obvious answer is that sharing burdens provides the greatest evidence we have of our transcendence—that is, our capacity to stretch beyond ourselves, and exist beyond ourselves, in the concerns of others. We act in love and concern—even when we have hardly anything to gain personally. What moralists call "altruism" is not the motive; it's the result. The ability to give ourselves and lose ourselves for the sake of another proves we are inherently designed to stretch beyond our own narrow frontiers. Sometimes I act because it makes me feel good; but when I carry the burdens of another, the purpose is not to improve the way I feel, but to extend myself (often without any feelings of return or compensation) beyond myself in love.

In a world intoxicated by romantic images of love, it probably is the love of a parent, done simply for the child, which is the clearest image of what love should be. The Scriptures give us occasional images of God as a lover or bridegroom; more often, though, especially in the teaching of Jesus, God is shown as a parent, a loving Father. Why? Because parents stretch beyond themselves for the good of their children even at the cost of themselves. A self-centered parent is, almost by definition, unable to be a parent in any significant sense.

The second reason why carrying the burdens of another advances humanity is harder to see but also quite undeniable. Somehow the very sharing of pain reduces the pain. Somehow the very accepting of another's hurt brings a greater wholeness.

We have trouble seeing this because, as moderns, we deal with pain very often from a technological perspective: It's a problem to be solved. Our attitude is: Study the situation, find the chemicals or formula, and then the solution to pain will appear. Although very few religious traditions stand against modern medicine, in whole or in part, most followers of Jesus see the medical profession as a profound way to serve, a way in which God works in the world. But in spite of what medicine can do, we are often called in life to carry the burdens of others when there is no technological or scientific solution. We simply accompany other in hurt. And that, in itself, somehow lessens the burden.

The great songs of Isaiah about the Suffering Servant have long intrigued those who have read and studied them. What is striking about them is the vicarious nature of the Servant's work.

The Servant literally suffers what the people are suffering, even to a higher degree, and brings wholeness to the people because of this. "By his bruises we are healed," Isaiah sings (Isa 53:5). Whereas many scholars believe the Servant is an image of the Jewish people themselves in their acceptance of the three-generation suffering of their exile, many more see the Servant as a unique figure, mysterious, but all the more compelling because of the mystery. Christians early on read the Servant of Isaiah as an anticipation of the work of Jesus Christ. When the Father speaks over Jesus, at his baptism, "This is my Son, the beloved, with whom I am well pleased" (Matt 3:17), it is a direct allusion to the Suffering Servant. (See Isaiah, chapters 42—53 for the various classic Servant passages.)

Indeed, if pain and brokenness isolate us, and if the violence of others makes us into things, then carrying the burdens of another affirms the two central points of our human value: (1) our connectedness and (2) our human reality. Simply not abandoning others in their hurt, simply opening ourselves up to the cries of others, affirms what is deepest about ourselves in the face of the greatest threat. It says that we are not alone. And it says that our value lies in our living itself, and not in our usefulness as an object in some scheme. In spite of breakdown, hurt, shame, and even death, when we carry each other's burdens we join in that great affirmation of our humanity which God endorsed in creating and redeeming us by carrying our suffering in Jesus Christ.

Burdens in the "Micro" World

In one way, the easiest burdens for us to carry are those right in front of us, in the lives of the people we are closest to. Many times, easing the pains of those we love consoles us, even if it doesn't thrill us. Mothers kiss the "boo-boos" of their children when they fall or bump themselves. Husbands and wives take on extra labor to pay tuition or provide for a household need that will not come otherwise. "I don't mind," they say, "It's for something important." The nobility of a husband caring for a dying wife, or a wife supporting a disabled husband in his prime years, forces the most cynical of hearts to reflect. We'll stretch ourselves because a relative or friend asks us something, even if it's something we'd rather not do.

Yet in subtle ways carrying the burdens of others on the "micro" level of our direct personal connections can be the most difficult of all burdens to deal with. Why? Because people take each other for granted and, with time and indifference, even those we live with can become no more than fixtures in our lives. The marriage will start out intense and focused. Every change of the newlywed's mood is read by the other. Each member of the couple goes out of the way to please the other. That's how it starts. After time, however, each of the couple starts making excuses for absences. Meals get perfunctory. Yet more time goes to outside hobbies. One party tries to express feelings to another, only to find deaf ears. The other party grows restless hearing of the needs of the other. "Don't be so needy; don't crowd me all the time!"

What kind of vulnerability and openness to the other makes ongoing communication possible, allows people to carry the burdens of another—and to do so consistently, for the short and long run? Only the openness that comes from living out with our very selves a pledge we have made to another. And when that is done in the context of our common journey toward God's fullness, it has the power of the Gospel—the openness that mirrors the love God has shown us.

That self-giving love, with no other end than what is good for the other, can help husband and wife cling to each other in fidelity; it can also be the glue that holds families together, even in times of transition. It binds together the "micro" world of our immediate relationships—family, friends, neighbors—in a way that counteracts life's indifference.

No one has explained the teenage years; some have argued that this ever-growing span of life was invented after the Second World War as a semi-permanent state of immaturity. However, what characterizes these years is more than hormonal change and bodily growth. A new kind of independence on the part of youth emerges, one that can—and often does—lead to isolation. Youth pout and sulk. Parents find it easier to disappear rather than put up with the awkwardness of these years. Dad is in the workroom fixing something; mom is at the parents' club making cakes. The children largely prefer it this way because they can be left to the world of their peers, one largely created by media and the blandest public opinion. So deadlocked does this situation become that children often have to "act out" through outrageous behavior just to get noticed. Unfortunately, it's often only when it's too late that parents realize that their child has been behaving strangely, or friends realize that one of their own has gotten in trouble.

A lived discipleship in the home, with regular prayer, communal sharing based on the Scriptures and personal lives, acknowledged values, and a healthy sense of forgiveness, would provide the perspective to consistently listen to those we love—because it creates a forum for people to communicate the sweet and the bitter. The common discipline of hearing and living the Word of God would protect the most vulnerable of those we love by forming a framework for our actions in life. Such a discipleship would give us the power to bear the burdens of those most immediately in our lives, and to get an angle on the larger circles that make up daily life such as work, school, friends, recreation, church.

One thing is sure: The inability to carry another's burdens makes life unnecessarily more difficult for many people. We paradoxically create distances that blunt us to each other, all the while begging to be closer. The closeness of God's drawing near, into our homes and lives, dares the modern world to risk closeness too. And perhaps our homes and our friendships are where the risk needs most to be taken.

Burdens in the "Macro" World

On the larger field of life, that "macro" world where our many personal circles combine to form neighborhoods, cities, nations, and cultures, we can likewise experience much frustration. As in the "micro" world, plain ignoring the world around us can be one cause for the frustration—the world just drifts by as if on a distant screen. But added to that are our feelings of inadequacy when trying to face the huge problems of society—labor, economy, justice, social values, poverty, racism, war, pollution, and the state of mother earth. Although people are barraged every day with information about these things, the very quantity of information makes them feel often *more* incapable of doing anything about this larger world.

Christian churches have had much to say concerning these larger issues. Some of this stems from matters that the early church faced, notably how to survive in a hostile society and how to serve in its social structures, particularly the military, with faith and integrity. Later, as Christian societies were formed, Christians experienced tremendous conflict at times between what a ruler wanted and what a church leader said was right. In more recent centuries, the overt poverty of people has called for policies about the dignity of the laborer and the care of migrants. Church leaders have responded to huge worldwide wars by articulating principles of a just war, of nuclear restraint and disarmament, and supporting multinational forums to prevent war. Arguing for the dignity of every human being, and the inherent rights of people, because of their humanity itself, to shelter, food, education, religious freedom and a living wage, the Church has painted a vision of life that anticipates the kingdom of God that Jesus inaugurated. These concerns, as much as any others, have consumed the attention of all the recent popes.

Yet some of this social teaching can make believers uneasy. "They should stay in the pulpits and leave worldly things to us," is one often-made response. After all, believers espouse many different social philosophies that, in themselves, are not sinful or wrong. Some favor labor, others management. Some insist on fiscal restraint while others believe that societies should be willing to spend resources, particularly on those deemed "deprived." Some naturally tilt toward order, others toward freedom and experimentation. For all those who favor big government, others will favor the least amount of government necessary.

Does the Gospel, then, enforce a particular economic or civic philosophy upon us? In this swirl of competing tendencies, where does a disciple who dwells in the Word of God take a stand? People on the left, and those on the right, can each cite their favorite scriptural passages.

When Jesus withstood the challenge of his opponents who were baiting him about paying taxes, simply uttering, "Give therefore to the emporer the things that are the emperor's, and to God the things that are God's" (Matt 22:21), he set forth an approach that allows disciples to work out complex issues that affect the "macro" systems of our lives. For the "emperor" side of our lives will indeed be complicated and changing—the social framework, the governmental systems, the economic theories, and scientific observations that form the world in which we discuss our public lives. But the "God" side of our lives should be simpler if only because, whatever our different philosophies, we have to read the Scriptures together and, together, be confronted by the vision of the kingdom that bears upon all of us, however much we might tilt to the right or the left.

Undoubtedly Jesus espoused no economic theories. But he did have some things to say about wealth. Living as he did on the care and donations of others, he obviously did not think that wealth in itself was evil. But the clinging to wealth in the face of the most direct needs that surround the rich seemed unintelligible to him. The stark contrast between the impoverished Lazarus who only wants scraps, and the wealthy head of the household who begrudges even this (Luke 16:20–31), has to make every disciple think twice. If wealth makes us closed and unresponsive in even a minimal way to the burdens of others, then our wealth does us little good, even in this life, let alone when we come to judgment.

Disciples have to work on both the "emperor" side of things through their attentiveness to the world, and on the "God" side of things through their attentiveness to the Word. But clearly the Word has priority over the world, not because it contains easily derived social formulas about poverty or economics (it doesn't), but because it brings the light and sensitivity that disciples need to reflect on the world. Our preoccupations with "the emperor," and all the various political or social ideas that we might entertain, can never outweigh our central preoccupation as disciples, God.

Every disciple also has to work out an approach to God and the world from the experience of active participation. The world can be changed only by working to change it. Sitting back and watching only makes for greater passivity and more frustration. But active participation in church, in the local community, and in the larger network of our churches and dioceses does make a difference because, through these, dramatic efforts can be made to lift the burdens of others. Youth groups, social services, soup kitchens, AIDS initiatives, schools, hospitals, and hospice programs are only some of the ways that the church responds to the macro challenges of bearing the burdens of others. Reaching out to those on the margins in our parish communities, to immigrants entering society, to those most vulnerable today (youth and the elderly) test well the sincerity of our discipleship. Even more than writing a check (though that, too, is certainly good), exposing our hearts to the sufferings and needs of others, without any expectation of a medal in return, is an indispensable way to grasp the kind of love that God shows us in Jesus Christ.

We have all smiled at the moral of the Christmas hymn, "The Little Drummer Boy," that teaches that each of us, however little we think we have, has plenty to give. Without losing that lesson, another lesson must also be memorized by those who follow Jesus: Of those to whom more has been given, more will be expected (Luke 12:48). Those with greater resources will, as a result, face a keener judgment. No wonder many a saint preferred to give away all possessions! It is, indeed, difficult for the wealthy to see the kingdom, let alone enter it (Matt 19:23).

The life of Dorothy Day, which spanned most of the twentieth century, perhaps displays what being a living witness to the Gospel by carrying the burdens of others can mean in a life. This, not so much in her eccentricity, for she appeared to many people as a strange person; nor even in the intensity of her life, although that intensity haunted her and those around her. More, Dorothy Day stands as an example of someone who, when she finally realized that the quest for God alone made sense of her life, began to find God everywhere, but most especially in the poor, the homeless, the unemployed, and the dejected. She stood up to any questioning of God's presence in the lowliest, whether that came from her friends or from church leaders. Blending deep prayer with deep social involvement, she spoke a coherent message of peace and inclusion. Along with a close circle of associates, she gave witness to a radical and powerful gospel message during years when American society would just as soon as brush away the difficult. As she herself put it, "If I have achieved anything in my life, it is because I have not been embarrassed to talk about God." And to live for God.

The grace to speak up. To not to be embarrassed. To see the connections between God and others and world. To live and proclaim those connections. To be living Gospels by bearing the burdens of others. What if all disciples knew they had the same gift from God?

Questions for Reflection

In your observation, how do people today navigate between the claims of being in community and the desire for individual space? Do you see much evidence of individualism? What signs of community do you observe?

What kinds of burden sharing do you see around you? In your experience, what effect does carrying the burdens of another have? Have you ever been consoled in a moment of pain? What were the dynamics?

What does it mean that God would take on our pain in Jesus Christ? What does this say about God's relationship to us? How does this change the way we experience our own lives?

What are the difficulties of loving others in the "micro" world of our personal lives? How can the Gospel help overcome these?

What changes in larger society do you think the Gospel has the power to bring? Can you think of ways that the Gospel has already brought change to society?

What do you think the Gospel is asking of those who have economic resources? What do you think is the best way to address the problems of the poor and oppressed? What do you think of the Church's effort to address social needs?

Developing Our Discipleship

Review how we attend to those around us, with a special awareness of our own obtuseness. Decide on changes that will allow us to relate more directly with those in our immediate circle. Explore patterns of noncommunication and isolation in our family? Can these be changed? Can help be gotten to open up communication?

Identify people whom we regularly ignore and try to discover the reason. Develop a plan to create access to these people and to become open to them.

Review the forms of discipleship in our households or our immediate circles. What are the levels of prayer and sharing? Are people able to reveal their burdens? What can make the sharing of burdens go better?

Evaluate how informed you are about the larger world in which you live. Do you evaluate the avenues of information in a critical way? How susceptible are you to ideologies and axe grinding? What can help you be better informed?

Periodically review your own politics, not just in terms of your natural associations (i.e., how you were raised or your social position in life), but in terms of the goals of the kingdom of God and the dignity of every person. Whatever your persuasion, how do your opinions and attitudes get rounded out to address the full range of humankind's needs?

What is your own personal investment in pursuing justice, peace, and the dignity of all?

What responsibilities do your possessions lay on you?

Exploring the Scriptures

Read how the Jewish people reasoned out their social relations in the light of their experience of God's revelation. See Deuteronomy 24:5–21.

Read the denunciations of Israel in Joel 2.

Reflect on 1 John 3—4, particularly for the way in which God's love is revealed by the way we treat each other.

Read the farewell discourse in John's Gospel (13—17) for the attitude of Jesus as servant and model; note the role of the Holy Spirit in Christian life.

Mapping the Disciple's Path

God's Word and our worship draw us together into community.

The Good News, witnessed and proclaimed by disciples,
bears upon our personal and our collective lives.

Our bondedness to others ties us to their lives.

It lays upon us the opportunity and obligation
to lessen their burdens
by helping to carry them as a demonstration
of the presence of the kingdom.

Disciples, resisting individualism, participate actively
in the transformation of the world.

Keeping God's kingdom as the perspective
from which all is weighed,
disciples serve God's vision of humankind.

These efforts remind disciples of their constant state:

Pilgrims who must always continue on the journey.

Chapter Seven

You Shall Continue on the Journey of Faith

What do you ask of us, O Lord?

"Who among you would say to your slave who has just come in from plowing or tending sheep in the field, 'Come here at once and take your place at the table'? Would you not rather say to him, 'Prepare supper for me, put on your apron and serve me while I eat and drink; later you may eat and drink'? Do you thank the slave for doing what was commanded? So you also, when you have done all that you were ordered to do, say, 'We are worthless slaves; we have done only what we ought to have done!'" (Luke 17:7–8)

"Take my yoke upon you, and learn from me; for I am gentle and humble in heart, and you will find rest for your souls. For my yoke is easy, and my burden is light." (Matt 11:29–30)

Whatever one may think of expectant mothers who play Bach or Beethoven on speakers close to their wombs while their children are maturing toward birth—thinking that they'll raise their children's IQ—no one can doubt that human learning begins almost immediately after birth. We are amazed that a child, hardly born, begins responding immediately to instincts. Noises, shapes, changes in light, smells, and touches come together to form, with astonishing speed, the familiar world of an infant. Friends are chagrined when, upon picking up a baby, the infant seems to automatically recoil because it has already learned so well the world of the mother. In such a short amount of time, the child has so learned the mother's world that it flinches from the stranger's. It can tell one environment from another.

Mothers, too, learn the different cries that their babies quickly develop, with one saying "I'm hungry," another "I want attention," and yet a third cry "I'm uncomfortable." This shows how quickly infants begin to collect aspects of their sensory world into patterns that make so much sense that they can communicate to their mothers their different needs.

Upon this instinctual intelligence a whole way of learning develops. The cooing of the parents becomes the stammering sounds of the little child. The hazy visual shapes become recognizable forms to which the baby responds with sharpness. The baby knows the mother, the father, the family members with a recognition that even modern computers cannot yet master. Pieces of songs, patterns of light, the difference between a smile and a frown, the alternate feeling of hard and soft shapes, multiple tones of voices—these and so much other sensory data become the base of a child's intelligence, it's ability to know the world.

Parents are astonished at the growth of this intelligence, the ways the child is able to relate events to each other and, with time, even anticipate them. The slam of a distant car door that tells the child that someone, maybe daddy, has arrived. The insatiable curiosity of children in their twos. The ability, early on, to memorize songs, both words and tunes, and even vary them with practice. The child's recoiling in the presence of the parents' tense moments of anger with each other, even when nothing has been said. The mimicking of an older brother or sister followed by, surprise, a new innovation.

We hear children gurgling, performing practical experiments in human learning as they try out sounds and tones to see which ones might match the sounds that have surrounded them by birth. These experiments soon mature into language that, itself, becomes an instrument of learning as the child grasps what a question is and, as importantly, an answer. As the child experiments with sounds and words, it also risks behaviors, stumbling this way, crawling that way, touching every sort of thing, evolving a kind of grid in the mind to replicate the world it is exploring. It begins to distinguish between pleasure and pain, perhaps the initial seeds of what will become, with transformation, the masterpiece of moral discernment.

We are learners from our infancy—and learners throughout our life. For this reason, we can grasp our lives as a journey of learning, new discoveries wedded to past ones, greater and deeper patterns capturing and transforming earlier and more limited ones, in a process of trial and error which is wired into human experience as much as anything.

The journey, then, is one of deepening truth about ourselves and our world. Human life can be conceived as a path toward greater truth, with the learnings of one moment becoming the stones that extend the path further toward future discoveries. Try as people might, through the blunders of life, to stymie their progress on the path, still the human mind demands to know "what is there," to know reality as we are formed to grasp it. Some truth dawns upon even the most ornery of humans.

A Hard Path

But the path toward truth, toward the capacity to relate our experience into coherent patterns that correspond to the world around us, is hardly straight and smooth. Rather, because trial and error are the dynamics of the path, it calls for constant straining and exertion. Some of the greatest thinkers of the modern world have noticed that human intelligence is "self correcting," because it does look for coherence. It recoils from pieces that just do not fit, words that make no sense, events that disrupt the learnings of past events.

Such learning by trial and error, however, does not make for an easy journey. The mind constantly confronts what seems out of place, and constantly berates itself for the false ways it has put things as it seeks to learn better its world. So the child who did not know that the new dog would react in its own way and, therefore, was different from the toy doll it is used to playing with, becomes the teenager who sees that telling jokes about the personal life of another person is different than reading jokes in the comic books. Children, slowly weaned from the world of their families as they enter the larger cosmos of school and society, are practicing every other threshold of change that will call the human forward to something new. How to make the frightening familiar—without that lesson, how small our world must be.

And no learning is more difficult than that of human relationships because this demands that a person look consistently and deeply beyond his or her own world into the world of another, of many others, to learn and grow from their experience. That looking into the world of another also has its own rules, depending on the relational bonds that tie people together—parents, siblings, friends, good friends, people we love, all people. That discovery of the world of another allows for the discovery of value, *of the good*, which furthers not just our own lives, but the lives of others and—in its broadest vision—the lives of all.

The trial and error involved in growing in human relationship probably entails the greatest risk of all. Because here the trials can often be risks of our very person; and the errors can lead to the deepest pains in life. Here we are putting to the test the deepest values in our lives. What is truly for the good of ourselves...and the good of another? What is for the good of friends...and the good of those who seem not to be friends? What kinds of self-renunciation make possible the loving of another? Or the loving of all people?

This is exactly the path that Jesus asks his disciples to walk, the path of ongoing discovery of the love of others for their own sake. Another way to say this is: The discovery of how to love others with the love that God has—generous, nonmanipulative, free and liberating, constant, and conducive to the good of the other. All the patterns of human intelligence push toward this ultimate pattern: That pattern of Absolute Good which we call God, which Jesus called his Father, and which Jesus said was the goal of the path of following him, of being his disciples.

When we look at the drive inside our human lives, this Absolute Good seems like a power inherent in life, pulling us forward into a limitless future. Our desire itself for progress toward the Good is the graced gift of a God who is supreme love.

The Learning Experience

Christians who gather for worship hear, on a regular basis, the Gospel accounts which, from different perspectives, insert us into the constant learning experience that we call discipleship. A disciple, after all, is a pupil in apprenticeship to a particular master, and the disciples of Jesus are those who are in apprenticeship to him. What this means can be glimpsed by the stories of those who followed Jesus on a path that, as much as anything, is filled with trial and error.

Perhaps no Gospel writer has a colder eye on the process than Mark, the Gospel that scholars surmise was the one written earliest. Mark, who is anxious to present Jesus as the suffering Messiah who brings salvation through self-renunciation, continually contrasts the generous spirit of Jesus with the self-interested concerns of those who follow Jesus. In Mark's Gospel, after Jesus begins to clarify the murderous fate that awaits him in Jerusalem, the disciples of Jesus are presented as immediately talking about which one of them will be the greatest. Which ones will get the privileged positions in the new kingdom they supposed Jesus would bring in a political sense (see Mark 9:31–34)?

In Mark's Gospel, no one stars in the role of buffoon more than Jesus' prime disciple, Peter. Right after Peter is given the insight that Jesus is the Messiah, and Jesus teaches that being Messiah means going down a path of suffering and death, Peter is arguing with Jesus. There must be another way! This cannot be the way it is! And Jesus, calling Peter a "Satan," (that is, "a tempter" who would distract Jesus from the necessary path) rebukes him sharply (Mark 8:29–33).

Again and again we hear of Jesus teaching his disciples about personal sacrifice, marriage and divorce, the accumulation of riches, the need for forgiveness and forgiving, all to the astonishment of his followers who consistently miss the point. Mark seems to climax the dullness of the disciples when he shows Jesus crossing the lake with his followers, talking about the contrast between the leaven (that is, the teaching) of the Pharisees and himself—and the disciples simply do not get the point of what he is saying (Mark 8:15–21). With memories of multiplied loaves, they cannot see Jesus is talking about his way of life.

So the process of discipleship is a learning experience characterized by trial and error. This means, of course, that it is also characterized by forgiveness and reconciliation as Jesus repeatedly lays aside the blunders of his followers and, in reconciliation, invites them to a new and deeper vision of the ways of God. Jesus, reacting in a variety of ways to the foibles of his followers, still manages to lead them beyond these foibles onto a new level of discipleship. Patient, observant, interacting, chastising, gently suggesting, vociferously insisting, Jesus remains the long-suffering teacher of those he calls to be part of his company.

Modern disciples need to return to this trial-and-error path to God, particularly because, unique among all the two-thousand years of Christian generations, ours seems to have the hardest time with admitting error and failure. For some reason, failure is linked in the modern mind with shame; and shame appears to be the one feeling that people today must reject at any cost.

We know, by contrast, that learning a new language or new sport involves much trial and error. We are even anxious to hear about our errors and ask others to point out when we mispronounce something, or when we need to modify one or another technique. We take none of this personally unless, of course, we are made to feel shamed because we get an accent in the wrong place or a misstep causes our team to fall behind.

Has the process of following Jesus become primarily a path of shame, such that modern believers have to hide their sins and deny their foibles—rather than learn from them through admitting them and being invited beyond them? Have we made religion so peculiarly sensitive that, although we might confess anything freely in a self-help group or to a therapist, we cannot even admit to ourselves a religious failure, let alone confess our failures to another? Has the need for forgiveness and renewal become the most elusive value in today's Christian life?

Only a perspective that has forgotten the mercy of Jesus, and Christ's power over sin, can give sin and error the kind of disempowering force that it plays in the lives of so many disciples today. Only a view of discipleship that has forgotten about trial and error can be fixated more on the errors than the learnings that the Master would bring us to.

When God asks us to walk along the path of discipleship, and to continue on that path, God is inviting us to a long-range vision in which even our sins and failures are transcended in love. God invites us to the humble viewpoint that we are all far from the fullness of Absolute Love which is the horizon within which every disciple walks, but that this Love pulls us forward in spite of our errors and blindness every time we repent. Being on the path, and continuing on the path of discipleship, means that we know both how far we are from the kingdom—and also how closely the kingdom has come to us, and continues to bear down upon us as we learn to be children of God.

Being on the path means that the power of the Word, and the energies that come to us in the Holy Spirit when we dwell in that

Word, continue to enliven us at whatever step we might be taking on the way of discipleship. We will, of course, blunder, often deliberately so. But the Jesus who draws us to face these blunders, however uncomfortable, is the same Jesus who teaches his followers unlimited forgiveness. Belief in Christ's discipleship of mercy lets us acknowledge our sinfulness to God and others without shame, but with wisdom.

Another problem with grasping the pattern of forgiveness and reconciliation is that it seems, according to the teaching of Jesus, that our experience of mercy is wrapped up with our ability to show it. A servant who is forgiven all of a huge debt cannot, according to the parable of Jesus, bring himself to forgive the mere pittance that a fellow servant owes (Matt 18:21–34). Though God's love is absolute and God's mercy is prior to everything, it appears we can accept this mercy only when, even in a halting way, we are able to show mercy to another.

A woman, near death, refused the consolations of the chaplain. She would have nothing to do with God. When once the chaplain was able to speak to her, her bitterness unfolded the story of a son who married a woman against her wishes. She had never spoken to him since. Now, at death's door, the hardness of her anger made God's mercy seem impossible, unintelligible. Her path of discipleship, of learning God's way, was stifled. Unable to show mercy, she was unable to accept it either. The trial and error of our own lives should soften us to the trial and error of others; God's kingdom rests on forgiveness.

The kind of learning experience Jesus gives his disciples is quite subtle because it does more than deal with exterior behavior over which we, more or less, have greater control. Jesus, being the master of psychology that he is, forces the disciples to learn about interior behavior over which we have less control. In the Sermon on the Mount, after articulating the founding principles of the kingdom that call us to find happiness in simplicity and trust, Jesus proceeds to argue that his disciples have to have even greater holiness than that striven for by the prominent religious traditions around him, the Pharisees, Scribes, and religious leaders. More than murder, the disciple has to keep even from anger; more than adultery, the disciple has to learn how to muzzle lust (see Matt 5:20ff.). The disciple has to pursue God's way with a persistence that almost borders on the simplistic, cutting out what even nudges us toward sin (Matt 5:29ff.).

Hardly a Lost Cause

As we contemplate the road that Jesus sets out for us, with the discipline necessary to maintain the journey, we may well be tempted to lose heart. "This is a lost cause," we may well begin to think, because the process of trial and error, of coming to forgive, and plumbing the depths of our motivation, make it look like sin and failure will never be eradicated from our lives.

How sobering to realize that even in the writings of the earliest Christians, whose fervor we imagine was intense and whose motivation absolutely perfect, we see that, after their conversion, they were still prone to sin. How often does Paul talk about the pettiness and sin of the members of his congregations, pointing out their lack of love (1 Cor 13) and the tendency of the young to commit scandalous sins (1 Cor 6:13–18)? He rails at the Corinthian community which has not the moral fiber to discipline someone committing a sin that should have sent shock waves through its members; he consigns this sinner to "Satan" hoping that the isolation will in some way lead to redemption (1 Cor 5:1ff.). In a subsequent letter to the Corinthians, however, he seems to forgive this sinner who outraged him (2 Cor 2:1–11), demonstrating that the process of sin-and-forgiveness continue through Christian life.

When Paul writes to the Galatians in what scholars believe to be a fairly early letter, he not only urges them to abide by the Holy Spirit (and its freedom), but points out the kinds of qualities, presumably rampant in the Christian community at Galatia, which accompany an absence of the Spirit even among the converted: "Now the works of the flesh are obvious: fornication, impurity, licentiousness, idolatry, sorcery, enmities, strife, jealousy, anger, quarrels, dissensions, factions, envy, drunkenness, carousing, and things like these. I am warning you, as I warned you before: those who do such things will not inherit the kingdom of God" (Gal 5:19–21). In addressing the sins of the Galatians, Paul is using what became a standard way of argumentation, developing a list of vices and sins, which early Christians would apply to the baptized as well as the unbaptized (cf. Matt 15:19, Rom 1:29, 1 Cor 6:9–10, Col 3:5, and the passage from Galatians).

What, then, is the point of conversion, of the coming of the Holy Spirit, of the life of discipleship if, indeed, the road which Jesus asks us to tread still holds the same pitfalls? Is there no difference between the converted and the unconverted? Does not sin hold a sway in both their lives? Is not, then, discipleship a lost cause? Any of us who have struggled to put aside sin for years, only to have it emerge later in life when we thought it was over, knows the difficulty of continuing on the path of what God expects of us.

Nevertheless, a believer sees a decisive difference between sins committed before conversion and sins done after conversion. Every disciple knows, at least instinctually, the power of the Holy Spirit that takes hold of a person's life after baptism. Before conversion, sin simply holds sway over us, perhaps causing some personal disquiet; but it is hardly seen for the evil and betrayal that it is. "Boys will be boys," we say; "Girls just want to have fun." Before conversion, sin calls for no discipline except, perhaps, that of discretion, to keep the sinner from public embarrassment or scorn. Before conversion, the force of sin in our lives is such that we rarely give it a second thought; it is part of our nature.

Conversion, however, places sin in a radically new context: It is named, identified, rejected, and, again and again, fought against. Sin still has the seed of power, but now a greater power looms, that of the Spirit of God that refuses to tolerate sin—and even fights the impulses that lead to sin. To commit a fault and just shrug it off, the state of the unconverted, clearly differs from what disciples do after conversion. They attend to a fault as soon as it happens, bringing it to the scrutiny of prayer and reconciliation, seeking advice from trusted guides about how to defeat the sin that plagues their lives. Disciples experience a forgiveness that announces liberty from sin's dominion and gradually, with discipline, frees us from sin's sway.

Only deluded Christians think they have no sin or that, once converted, they cannot sin (mistakenly interpreting 1 John 3:9). The experience of every Christian denomination recognizes that those who have converted still sin, and the Church must deal with that. Some call it "backsliding." Some ostracize sinners. But centuries of experience in the Spirit have lead Catholics, Orthodox, and some other mainline Protestant communions, to the discipline of confession which, recognizing the continued power of sin in our lives, defeats that power through humility, openness, trust, assurance of mercy, and the bestowal of the Spirit in forgiveness.

To the End

God asks that we, as disciples, continue on the journey of faith to the end. God calls us not to be waylaid by our weaknesses, foibles, and sin. Even more, God strengthen us, giving us the resources for the road by raising our eyes to the vision of heaven—which is the perspective in which all the steps of this journey on earth must be seen. Again and again he teaches his disciples the quality of perseverance, of the bridesmaids who stay watching through the night (Matt 25:1–13), or the laborers who do not give up when the Master delays but keep on being vigilant (Matt 24:42ff.). Having undertaken Christ's journey, how is it possible to look back (Luke 9:62)? The letter to the Hebrews, which gives every evidence of being written to a congregation that was tested and tempted to give up, thinks nothing can be worse than abandoning the pursuit of God's kingdom (Heb 10:26–27).

The ancient Hebrew people were faced with the same temptation. Having escaped from Egypt, trudging through the desert, unsure of where God was leading them, they gave into the temptation to believe that God would not care for them in their hunger or thirst. They longed for the "flesh pots" of Egypt because having food in slavery was better, they surmised, than dying of hunger in freedom (Exod 16:3). The Hebrew Scriptures returned many times to reflect on the hungers of the desert, particularly on the mistrust that lay behind that hunger.

Perhaps for this reason Christians, seeing their discipleship as a journey, have particularly rejoiced in the holy Eucharist, the celebration of Christ's true and continuing presence with his people through the sacrament of food and drink. This is food for the pilgrim, Christians have concluded, the necessary sustenance of God's presence made real in the sacrament of union, if Christians would not lose heart and give up the journey. The regular worship of God in the Eucharist, at least weekly (and for many disciples a daily recourse) provides the spiritual food of God's Word and Christ's risen presence which make the journey bearable. The ancient name for communion given to the dying is "viaticum"—a popular way of saying that the Lord is with us "on the way."

Those who most mock the Christian way of life, it may be argued, are those who, calling themselves Christian, take the least advantage of the resources God has given for the journey of discipleship—starving themselves by their absence from the Eucharist and deluding themselves into thinking that, with occasional memories of God, they can persevere to the end.

Statistics about participation in worship across Christian believers show that, on any given Sunday, roughly less than 40% of worshippers will make it to church. This statistic includes some groups that have higher attendance, meaning that many churches have many empty pews. That is a lot of hungry people who think they can attain the kingdom without being fed.

"You shall not give up on the journey of faith, but you shall continue on the path," God says, for otherwise we betray the path by saying that life has nowhere to go. Staying where we are, keeping up with those around us, amusing ourselves for the years that are given to us, palliating our pains with little bromides—this is all many believers think they need to do. At least that is what their behavior is saying. A quick scan of history, as well as today's popular culture, shows, however, this Christian skimpiness as an empty alternative to the Christian's real journey—a nonpath that does go nowhere.

But if we are faithful to the passion that is built into us by our births, our coming to know and our desire for truth, our ongoing learning and self-correction, our limitless questions, and, most of all, our drive for Absolute Love, then the limited vision of get-what-you-can simply cannot satisfy us. Only a vision of the banquet, of the bridal feast in which all are joined in the depth of God's love, unendingly, fits the hungers of spirits like ours (Rev 21:1ff.). Captured by the grace of God's love, we are forever longing for the completion of that love.

This is exactly the vision that Jesus gives his followers. Indeed, as the time of his own death draws near, Jesus piles on the images of the banquet feast and the wedding party (Matt 22:2ff.; Luke 14:15ff.) to provide just a glimpse of what the journey is all about. The Book of Revelation, so filled with strange imagery, ends with an image that seems to combine the greatest longings of the prophets for a kingdom in which God would be the community's light and life with the imagery of the bridegroom which Jesus himself gave us (Isa 60: 19; Rev 21:1ff., 21:23). For in the kingdom that all true disciples long for, there is no more pain or weeping. In the kingdom that Jesus inaugurates, there is no need for moon or sun or any "physical" light because God will be transparent light, illuminating the kingdom with a directness and intimacy that will make the sun, metaphorically speaking, look dim.

Behind every temptation to fall away lies the primal temptation to substitute something else for the kingdom, to dwell in something other than God's Word, to settle for a smaller and seemingly more manageable vision. Behind every wandering from the path lies the all too instinctual desire to create our own rules, our own universe, in place of accepting God's rule of love and life, the commandments of discipleship. Behind every stumbling on the path lies the preference of our will to God's gracious will of love. When God commands the disciples of Jesus to continue on the path, God insists that we keep the image of heaven, of life's completion and earth's fulfillment, as the ultimate viewpoint of our lives. God calls us to resist any impulse to settle for less, to settle for ourselves rather than Absolute Love.

For discipleship teaches us that we are made for just such a kingdom—where the hopes that our hearts cannot repress finally passes from dream to reality, where the path that Christ's disciples have trod with so much difficulty suddenly slips into the promised land, and we are, at last, at rest.

Questions for Reflection

Would you describe life as growth, a moving forward? What is your own experience of human personal growth? Growth in intelligence? Growth in human relationships? Growth in moral awareness and depth?

What is the process of trial and error in human learning? Do you think of moral behavior, learning to reflect the good completely in our own actions, as something that can be learned, and improved by learning?

What do you think is behind the reluctance of people to address their particular sinfulness today? Why so much sharing with therapists or self-help groups, but so little enthusiasm for confessing sin? What is the role that shame plays in moral thinking? What role should it play?

What goals do you think people live for today most deeply? Do you think people have a sense of an unending destiny? Are people attracted to the prospect of Absolute Love and unending life? Why or why not?

What is your vision of heaven? Which of the biblical images of heaven help you imagine God's promise best?

Developing Our Discipleship

Determine your short- and long-term goals; what priorities do these have in your life? Why? Share these goals with someone important to you.

Try to summarize for yourself what you believe the ultimate goal of life is, both within our experience now and in the future of God.

What is your own discipline concerning trial-and-error? Examine your life on a regular basis. Bring that examination to a trusted friend, counselor, and confessor. Develop a plan of regular review and confession.

What has blocked you from showing mercy? What has caused this block? Can it be overcome?

Determine what is the pattern of your greatest temptations. Explore how these distract you from your path of discipleship.

Regularly explore the features of your image of heaven—the people associated with it, the feelings, the sense of time.

Figure out ways to support others on their journey of faith, particularly those who are in doubt.

Commit yourself to maintaining the on-going place of worship for you on the path of discipleship.

Exploring the Scriptures

Read that primal "journey story" in the Scriptures, the call of Abraham in Genesis 12.

Reflect on the journey through the desert after the escape from Egypt in Exodus 15:22—17:7.

Feel the excitement of the return of the Jewish people from exile in Babylon in Isaiah 45, and the hope of the returned exiles in shown in the book of Ezra.

Scan the book of Acts to see the travels of the early followers of Jesus; see the movement from Jerusalem to Rome, and the shift from stories of Peter and Stephen, to stories of Paul and Barnabas.

Read Paul's account of his own journeys in 2 Corinthians 11:23–28.

Explore the final chapters of Revelation with its vision of the new Jerusalem.

Mapping the Disciple's Path

The distance between ourselves and the call of God's Word
makes us permanent pupils.

Because we are always learning, trial and error
form the texture of our lives.

Disciples, therefore, live through the experience
of forgiveness and reconciliation.

The mercy of reconciliation can be accepted only to the extent
that a disciple shows mercy.

The progress on the journey toward Absolute Love entails
the constant battling of sin.

This means that disciples need the resources of the sacraments,
of prayer, and of the Spirit
if they would persevere on the journey.

The experience of forgiveness and the celebration
of Eucharist anticipate the
unending banquet that awaits us when the kingdom is fulfilled
and our journey is complete.